INSECTS AND THEIR WORLD

Of all the animals that live on our earth, insects are the largest group. They also are among the most varied and interesting.

Insects and Their World introduces us to these abundant creatures. It tells how insects are built, how they grow up, and where they make their homes. We meet young mosquitoes that swim and crickets that burrow. We discover that moths find their mates by smell, while fire-flies use eyes and built-in flashlights. One butterfly will spend the winter asleep, while another will migrate thousands of miles, as birds do, to find warmer weather. We find that some insects have lived without much change since the Coal Age, a quarter-billion years ago. Others have adopted new habits, homes, and foods since man began to build houses and towns.

These are just a few of the fascinating facts in this survey of the insect world. To it, the authors bring the viewpoint and method they used with outstanding success in *Birds and Their World*. Insects are treated as living things, not museum specimens. Each subject is intro-duced by a story that shows some insect in a vital activity. This is followed by a discussion, also centered upon typical insects which young readers may find and watch.

Insects and Their World

By CARROLL LANE FENTON and
DOROTHY CONSTANCE PALLAS

Illustrated by Carroll Lane Fenton

The John Day Company   New York

Contents

Aster, the black swallow-
tail butterfly.

Getting
ready to
become a
chrysalis.

Caterpillar feeding

Chrysalis

How a caterpillar became a chrysalis
and then a butterfly.

Growing Up in the Insect World

ASTER crawled along the edge of a parsnip leaf. Soon he stopped and began to eat. *Nip-nip-nip* went his jaws as he cut off juicy bits of leaf and chewed them until they were soft.

The gardener who owned the parsnips called Aster a worm, but he really was a caterpillar. That difference was very important. Worms are wriggly creatures that never become anything else, no matter how long they live or how large they grow. But caterpillars are young insects that turn into moths or butterflies. When Aster grew up, he would be a big black butterfly with yellow and blue markings. Each of his hind wings would also have an orange spot with a black center, and a "tail" almost a half inch long. It would explain the butterfly's everyday name, which is black swallowtail.

Caterpillars are often called worms because they crawl and have wriggly bodies. Aster also had many short legs, just as some worms do. The first three pairs of legs were near his head; they were jointed and ended in claws. Next came four pairs of baby legs, or prolegs, which were thick and soft. So were the two prop legs at the hind end of Aster's body. Both prolegs and prop legs ended in claspers that had tiny hooks. These hooks were just right for holding to stems or leaves.

7

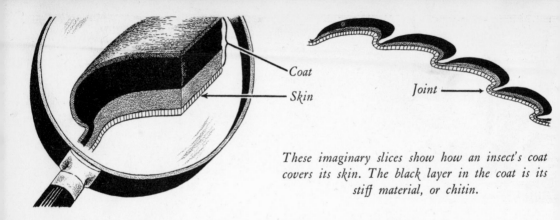

These imaginary slices show how an insect's coat covers its skin. The black layer in the coat is its stiff material, or chitin.

Aster had hatched from a yellow egg which his mother laid early in June. At first he was black with a broad white spot near the middle of his body. Six rows of spines ran along his back and sides.

Like all young caterpillars, Aster needed a great deal of food. He ate until it seemed he would burst—and at last he did. First he spun a little pad of silk on his parsnip leaf and held tightly to it. Then he bent his body until the skin seemed to split down the middle of his back. Actually, the thing that split was a tough outer cover which Aster's skin had built up around his body. Scientists have named this cover the cuticle (kyu′ ti kul), but we may call it a coat. All insects have these skin-made coats. Many of them are much thicker and harder than the coats of caterpillars.

Soon after Aster's old coat split, he wriggled and crept out of it. He also filled his body with air. His skin had begun to form a new coat that was much larger than the old one. In order to fill this brand-new coat, Aster had to make himself bigger by swallowing air. But soon he felt hungry and started to eat. In three days he ate and grew so much that he had to change coats again.

A young water bug (right) has become larger since it crawled out of its old coat (left).

When a growing insect sheds its coat, we say that it molts. Most caterpillars molt four times, and that is what Aster did. Many caterpillars also change their colors—and Aster did that, too. After losing one spiny black-and-white skin, he came out in a new one that was smooth. It was bright green, with black stripes that ran around his body. Spots on the black stripes were yellow.

One morning a robin flew down to the parsnip where Aster was feeding. Robins often catch caterpillars, but this one did not harm Aster. The caterpillar raised his head with a jerk as two pockets in his skin turned inside out. In a moment they became orange-colored "horns" that gave off a very bad odor. The robin knew that Aster tasted badly, too, so she hopped away to find some other food.

When Aster had grown as much as he could grow, he lost his appetite. He also felt restless and began to crawl. He went from one parsnip plant to another, as fast as he could go. At last he stopped on the lower part of a leaf and put his head against the stem.

The caterpillar seemed to be resting, but he really was spinning silk. It was made in a gland inside his body and came out

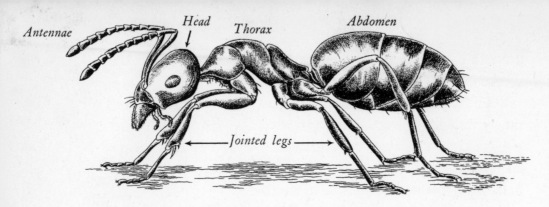

Antennae   *Head*   *Thorax*   *Abdomen*

←——— *Jointed legs* ———→

This ant shows the parts of an insect's body.

through a tube in his lower lip. At first the silk was clear and runny, like syrup, but it dried into a tough thread.

Aster moved his head to and fro as he spun, tangling the silk into a pad that was fastened to the leaf. Next he turned so his "tail" held to the pad. Last of all, the caterpillar spun a loop and put his head through it. The loop kept him from falling while he shed his old coat and came out in a new greenish-brown one that hardened into a case. Aster, the caterpillar, became a chrysalis (kriss' a liss).

Inside the hard chrysalis case, Aster's body softened and began to change. The changes went on for about nine days, and then the chrysalis case split open. When Aster wriggled out of it, he was a butterfly.

We often think of butterflies as quick-moving insects with bright-colored wings. But Aster was slow and dull, and his wings were soft, wet, crumpled pads. He hung from a leaf while they spread out and became stiff, and while the tiny scales that covered them dried. The dry scales gave Aster's wings their colors and made them look almost like velvet.

Aster became a butterfly, and butterflies are insects. We sometimes call all insects "bugs," but that is not correct. Bugs are one special group of insects, not the entire class.

Scientists have named about 700,000 kinds of insects. They range from gnats so small they can hardly be seen to moths with wings almost twelve inches wide. They live on land, in ponds, lakes and streams, and at the edge of the sea. Some insects even make their homes in plants or in animals.

You can tell insects by their jointed bodies, which are divided into three main parts called head, thorax, and abdomen (thoe′ raks, ab′ doe mun). Two "feelers," or antennae (an ten′ ee), grow out from the head, but the legs are fastened to the thorax. Full-grown insects always have six legs, but young ones such as caterpillars may have several more. Most grown-up, or adult, insects also have four wings or two, but some have none. The silverfish shown on page 67 is a wingless insect.

Dogs, birds, and many other creatures have bony skeletons inside their bodies. Bones keep these creatures in shape and enable them to move. When a dog runs, it shortens (or contracts) muscles that are fastened to jointed bones. A bird does the same thing when it flies or pecks at its food.

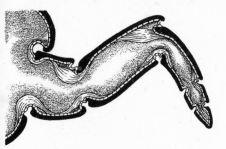

Muscles that shorten, or contract, move the sections of an insect's leg.

Muscles also move the jointed bones in an arm.

254

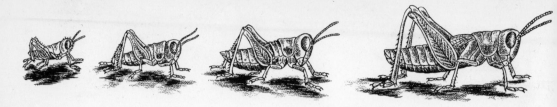

This young grasshopper changes a little at a time—

Insects have no bones, and their only skeletons are the coats that form around their skins. These coats may be thin and soft, like those Aster wore when he was a caterpillar. Coats also may be thick and hard, like the "shells" that cover many beetles, or the "case" Aster developed when he became a chrysalis.

The difference between soft coats and hard ones is produced by a substance called chitin (ky' tin). Aster's caterpillar coats were soft because they did not contain much chitin. His chrysalis coat, or case, was hard because it contained much more. So did the coat that covered his body when he became a butterfly. Chitin also stiffened the broad, thin wings with which the grown-up Aster flew.

If a stiff, hard coat were made in one piece, the creature inside it could not move. But an insect's coat is never made in one piece. It consists of many sections, or segments, held together by thin joints that bend easily. You can see these joints on a caterpillar's body and on the part of a chrysalis in which the abdomen develops. Joints also show plainly on the abdomen and legs of a butterfly, grasshopper, or cockroach. When an insect walks, its muscles move the sections of its legs, just as a dog's muscles move its bones.

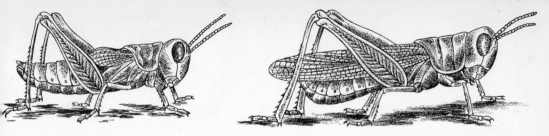

—as it goes through an incomplete, or gradual, metamorphosis.

Aster began life as an egg which his mother laid on a leaf. The egg hatched into a caterpillar that grew, changed into a chrysalis, and then became a butterfly. Scientists call this set of changes a complete metamorphosis. Metamorphosis (met′ uh mor′ fo sis) means a change in form and appearance. The word "complete" tells us that Aster went through all the changes any insect can make.

All butterflies go through a complete metamorphosis, and so do moths, wasps, and beetles. But many insects do not change so much. A grasshopper, for example, does not start out as a caterpillar or become a chrysalis. A baby grasshopper has head, thorax, abdomen, and legs; only its wings are missing. They develop after several weeks and then become larger and larger until the insect is full-grown.

This kind of change is called an incomplete, or gradual, metamorphosis. It is incomplete because it does not have all the stages that match the caterpillar and chrysalis. It is gradual because changes are made a little at a time, not suddenly, like the one that turned Aster into a chrysalis.

Now that we know how different insects grow up, suppose we use some more new words.

Young butterflies and moths are caterpillars. "Baby" flies are

13

called maggots, and young, wriggly beetles are grubs. But a name for all these creatures is larvae (lahr′vee), though a single one is a larva. These names fit all the wormlike young ones of insects that have complete metamorphosis.

Any young insect that changes gradually is a nymph (nimf). This name is borrowed from ancient goddesses that were supposed to live in trees, rivers, and hills. Some insect nymphs are beautiful, but others are ugly creatures. A nymph that lives in the water is often called a naiad (ny′ ad).

Aster became a chrysalis—but if he had been a moth we would call him a pupa (pyu′pa). Most chrysalids and pupae (pyu′ pee) do not move about or eat, for they are resting while they change into grown-up insects. Still, some pupae resemble adult insects, and mosquito pupae are able to swim and catch smaller creatures for food. Many people think these pupae are larvae of a special kind.

Some moth caterpillars crawl into the ground before they become pupae. Other caterpillars hide in corners where they will not be seen. Still others spin cases or cocoons of silk and become pupae inside them. You can find cocoons on trees, among weeds, or even in buildings. Small moths come from small cocoons, but big cocoons belong to moths that are large and beautiful.

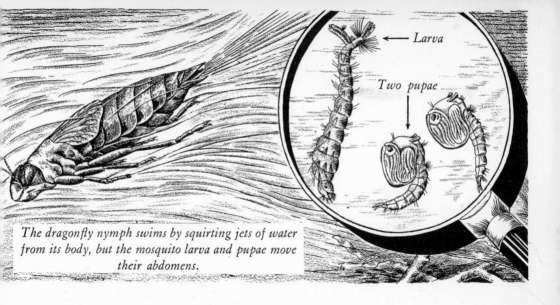

The dragonfly nymph swims by squirting jets of water from its body, but the mosquito larva and pupae move their abdomens.

— Larva

Two pupae

How Insects Move About

LIB, a dragonfly nymph, stood at the bottom of a pond. Her rough body and dull colors made her look like an old stick.

Although Lib was hungry, she did not hunt for food. Instead, she stood so still that other creatures did not see her. Soon a small tadpole wriggled toward her. Lib waited until it came quite close. Then she reached out with her long lower lip and pulled the tadpole into her mouth.

After Lib swallowed the tadpole she walked to another part of the pond. She moved slowly and carefully, putting her feet down one by one. Of course, walking spoiled the disguise that made her look like a bit of stick. A fish that saw Lib knew she was an insect and tried to swallow her.

There was no time for Lib to hide, and she could not run. But she was able to do something else that worked just as well. In her abdomen was an open place which people call the gill chamber. Lib used the gill chamber for breathing, and kept it full of water. But when the fish came toward her, she squeezed some muscles and forced the water out. As the water shot out, it pushed Lib forward so fast that the fish was left behind.

Dragonfly nymphs swim with jets of water, but many other insects use their abdomens or legs. Mosquito wrigglers, for example, often float near the surface, with their heads hanging downward. But at other times the wrigglers swim by jerking from one side to the other. A mosquito pupa can swim almost as well as a larva. But the pupa moves its abdomen forward and backward, not from side to side.

Water bugs have broad, flat bodies and swim with two long hind legs which can also be used for walking. The diving beetle's hind legs are flattened like oars and have hairy fringes which make them seem wider than they really are. Water boatmen and back swimmers row themselves about under water with still longer hind legs that have still wider fringes. All these insects are smooth, with streamlined bodies that slip through the water easily. This helps the insects capture food or escape from other creatures that try to catch them.

Most insects that live on land use their legs for walking, climbing, or jumping. Caterpillars, however, have such short legs that we say they crawl. Many of them resemble Aster, with six jointed legs near their heads and ten more along the rest of their bodies. This arrangement lets the creatures crawl without bending their bodies unless they want to turn.

The caterpillars called measuring worms, inch worms, or loopers are built on a different plan. They have six jointed legs close to the head and four or six prolegs near their tails. These caterpillars reach forward as far as they can and take hold of something. Then they pull the hind legs up until they almost touch the forelegs. This makes the caterpillars' bodies curve like the letter U turned upside down. They seem to be measuring the distance as they crawl along.

Some measuring worms are shaped and colored like stems of the plants on which they feed. When something disturbs these caterpillars, they raise their bodies and hide by standing still. Even hungry birds cannot tell them from short stems or twigs.

Two measuring worms, a swift ground beetle, and a slow-moving walking stick.

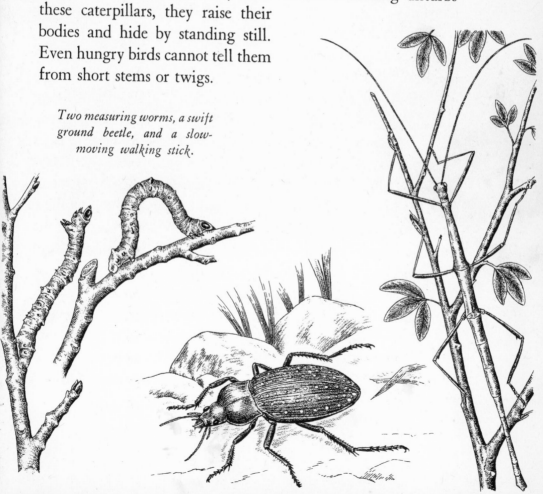

Measuring worms can crawl quite fast, but never as fast as the woolly bear (page 94). It is a hairy, reddish-brown and black caterpillar that stops eating in the fall and hurries around till it finds a place to hide through the winter. Woolly bears often crawl across pavements or sidewalks, going almost as fast as a person can walk.

Adult insects walk fast or slowly, just as caterpillars do. One of the slowest is the walking stick. Walking sticks are related to grasshoppers and crickets, but their bodies are very slender. They often walk so slowly that they hardly seem to move. When something alarms them, they stand as still as measuring worms.

Walking sticks feed upon leaves, which do not move about. But ground beetles eat other insects, and have to capture their food. A ground beetle's legs are long and strong, and can run rapidly.

Grasshoppers, crickets, and katydids have legs that are built for jumping as well as for walking or climbing. A grasshopper's hind legs are long, with strong muscles under their skins and hard coats. When these muscles straighten the legs with a sudden jerk, the insect leaps into the air.

Everyone who has watched grasshoppers knows that they also have wings and can fly. So do bugs, beetles, wasps, butterflies, and many other insects.

The grasshopper nymph on pages 12 and 13 shows how wings develop. When the creature hatches it does not have them, and it has to move about on its legs. Then pads of skin appear on the back, and wings begin to grow inside them. They get bigger each time the grasshopper molts, until they are fully grown.

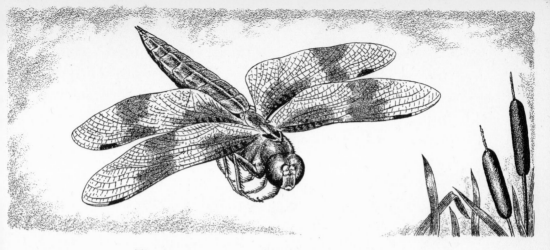

The dragonfly's wings spread out at each side. This is a skimmer related to Lib.

The wings of a butterfly or moth do not begin to develop until it becomes a chrysalis or pupa. We never see them until they are as large as they will ever become.

This does not mean that they are ready to use. When an insect comes from a pupa or makes its last molt, its wings are wet, crumpled things that have to spread out and dry. As the wings spread, their hollow veins harden. They become a framework that stiffens the wings and makes them strong, just as a framework of sticks gives stiffness and strength to a kite.

Mosquitoes and flies have only two wings, but most other insects have four. The wings also are built on four different plans.

The oldest, simplest plan is the one we see in dragonflies. A dragonfly's wings are long and stiff, and they spread out on both sides of the body. They stay there when the dragonfly rests, for they cannot be folded away.

Butterflies and some moths follow the second plan. Their wings are stiff, too, and spread sideways while the insects are flying. But when they rest, the wings come together in an upright position above the insects' backs.

Wings that work on the third plan fold down against the back. You can see this in most small moths, as well as in wasps, cicadas, bees, and many other insects. Even flies, which have only two wings, fold them against their backs.

The fourth plan is easily seen in beetles and grasshoppers. The first pair of wings has become a pair of shields or covers. The second pair of wings is thin, and can be spread out or folded up like an old-fashioned fan. When a beetle or grasshopper flies, it lifts its shields, spreads its hind wings, and beats them to and fro. When the insect alights, it folds its hind wings and covers them with the shields.

These three kinds of insects have wings arranged in different ways. The beetles' forewings have become shields for the hind wings.

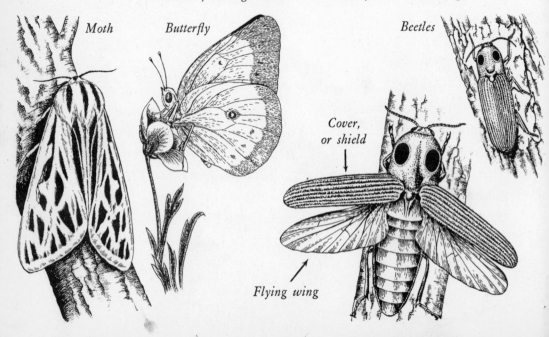

Moth   Butterfly   Beetles

Cover, or shield

Flying wing

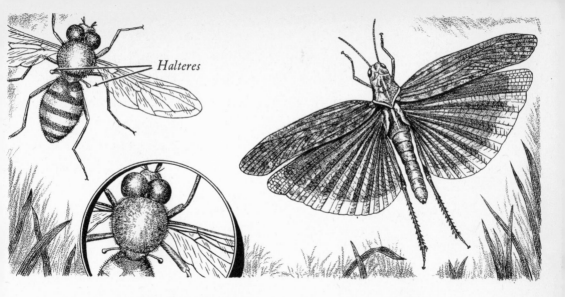

Flies keep their balance by moving two "halteres."
The grasshopper starts to fly by jumping.

We can easily tell that some insects fly better than others. Grasshoppers fly poorly, for they have to start out by jumping and they never go very far very fast. Dragonflies use their wings very well, for they can fly swiftly or slowly, dart up or down, and even "stand still" in the air. But flies and mosquitoes probably are the best fliers in the insect world. Their two wings seem to work better than four, for they can be moved up and down hundreds of times every second. This means that the insects can move very swiftly. Since they do not grow tired quickly, they often fly long distances.

Did you ever wonder how flies keep their balance? The explanation is in two little pegs with knobs on their ends. These pegs, which are called halteres (hal tee′ reez) bob up and down while the insects are flying, and keep them "on the beam."

Finding and Pleasing Mates

PROM crawled out of her cocoon on a sunny June morning. Her body was weak and wet, and her wings looked like tiny damp rags. She took a few steps and stopped on the under side of a twig. There she stayed while her wings spread out and became stiff. The long scales on her body dried out, too, till they looked like silky hair.

Some people who saw Prom called her a butterfly, but she actually was a moth. Her thick, "hairy" body showed that. So did her antennae, which were branched like tiny fern leaves. A butterfly's antennae are slender. Instead of having side branches, they are thickened at the end.

The kind, or species (spee' sheez), to which Prom belonged is called promethea (pro mee' thi uh). Prometheas come from brownish-gray cocoons that are spun inside curled-up leaves. Before the caterpillars spin their cocoons, they cover the leaf stems with silk and fasten them to twigs. Silk keeps the cocoons from falling or from blowing away.

Prom looked dull and ugly while she was wet, but she became beautiful when she dried. Her wings spread out till they measured four inches from tip to tip. Their fluffy scales turned reddish brown or formed markings of black, white, buff, and pale

22

*One female promethea moth has just come from her
cocoon, but the other's wings are fully spread.*

purple. They made Prom resemble another large moth whose
name is cecropia (si crow' pi uh).

Prom sat still for almost an hour after her wings and body
were dry. Then she flew to another part of the tree and hid
between two branches. There she stayed all afternoon and all
evening, until the sky became dark. Male prometheas fly about
in the late afternoon, but females like Prom always wait until
night.

Some female insects have to hunt for mates, going from one
place to another until they find some males. But Prom used an
easier method that worked just as well. As the sky grew dark,
she came out of hiding and fluttered from leaf to leaf. She also
sent out a message which said that a female promethea was wait-
ing for a mate.

When we human beings send messages, we put them into

words. But Prom was a moth who could not speak, and her message was an odor. It spread from her body into the air, and a breeze carried the odor-message for miles. Every male moth that smelled it started out to find Prom. Soon so many males were flying toward her that they seemed to be having a race.

The moth that won the race was young and handsome, but he did not look like Prom. His wings were smaller and narrower than hers, and his colors were much darker. His body had no white markings, and the branches of his antennae were wide. They were covered with tiny "smellers" which had sniffed Prom's odor and had told the male exactly where she was.

Prometheas belong to a group, or family, which we call silk moths. Their most famous member is the silkworm, which comes from eastern Asia. Their best-known American species are the promethea, cecropia, and polyphemus (pol″ i fee′ mus). The luna moth is pale green, but the polyphemus is tan or yellowish brown, with stripes and "eye spots" on its wings.

A male promethea and his broad, branched antennae.

Many butterflies and moths suck nectar, but silk moths do not. When they leave their cocoons they are strong enough to find mates, lay eggs, and fly about for a few nights. Then they die or become so weak that birds and other creatures catch them.

Short lives explain why silk moths try to mate on the first night after they leave their cocoons. On that night the males are still fresh and strong and can fly swiftly to the females. The females then have plenty of time to lay two or three hundred eggs on leaves which the larvae will be able to eat. Prom put her eggs on wild-cherry leaves, but other mother prometheas go to sassafras trees, sycamores, ash trees, or even lilac bushes. Leaves of all these plants are eaten by the larvae, which become blue-green caterpillars about two inches long.

.　　.　　.　　.

Insects have various ways of attracting and finding mates. Most moths and butterflies use odors, and so do many beetles. Male June "bugs" have big, branched antennae that smell the odors of females. But fireflies, which also are beetles, flash lights. This is specially important to species whose females have no wings. They climb weeds or blades of grass and sit there, flashing again and again. When a male sees one of these signals, he is almost sure to stop and make the female his mate.

Some scientists think crickets, kaytdids, and grasshoppers attract mates by singing to them. Since these insects cannot make sounds with their throats, they scrape their outer wings together. When field crickets do this they make chirping sounds, but tree crickets say "Chur-chur-churr." Katydids scrape out their name, but grasshoppers rattle, buzz, or call "P-zee, p-zee" loudly,

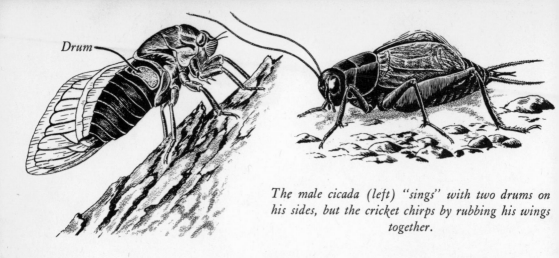

Drum

The male cicada (left) "sings" with two drums on his sides, but the cricket chirps by rubbing his wings together.

over and over again. Male cicadas have drumlike hollows in their abdomens. When muscles stretch the heads of those drums, they produce loud buzzing songs which we often hear on hot summer days. Female cicadas have no drums, and they never make a sound.

These insects *seem* to sing to their mates, but we are not sure that they do so. Several scientists say that male insects make loud sounds to keep other males away. And a few scientists think insects sing for both reasons. Perhaps a cricket's chirps ask females to hop over and see him, and at the same time tell males that they must not come near.

Many insects that cannot sing attract mates by showing off or dancing. The males of several tiny flies have bright colors that seem to please females. These male flies walk to and fro and show, or display, their colors. Other small insects do flying dances in order to attract the females. While the males dance, they give presents of food to the females, who hold their gifts while they mate. Even though these insects do not sing, they work very, very hard to please their tiny mates.

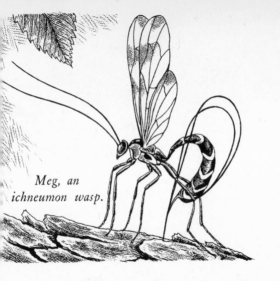

Meg, an
ichneumon wasp.

Horntail

Eggs *and How They Are Laid*

MEG flew across a meadow and into a grove. Soon she alighted on an oak tree and began to walk around its trunk.

People sometimes call Meg a fly, but her correct name is ichneumon (ik new′ mon) wasp. Flies never become as large as Meg, for her body was one and one half inches long. Flies also have only two wings, and Meg had four. Finally, flies have nothing like Meg's long "tail." It really was an egg-layer, almost three inches long. Meg used it to put her eggs in special places where the young ones would find food.

Meg was hunting for places to lay her eggs when she alighted on the oak tree. She walked up and down the trunk, but could not find what she wanted. Soon she flew to a willow, but it was no better than the oak. Meg left it and buzzed away to another part of the woods.

Meg was hard to please, but she could not help it. Her young ones would need a special kind of food, and she had to lay her eggs where they could get it. The food was grubs, or larvae, of an insect called the pigeon horntail. Horntail grubs feed upon wood, and make burrows or tunnels in trees as they eat it. Meg had to find horntail tunnels and lay her eggs in them, or her little ones would starve.

The fourth tree Meg visited was an old, dying elm. Its bark was beginning to fall off, and only one branch had leaves. Several horntail grubs were burrowing in its wood.

Meg did not know the grubs were there when she alighted on the tree. She found them by running along the branch, waving her antennae and tapping the bark. She seemed to be feeling, but she really was trying to smell the odor made by horntails. At last she found what she wanted. Meg stopped just above the grub's tunnel and bent her egg-layer into a loop. Then she began to push it through the dead bark and dry wood.

Meg's egg-layer had looked like a stiff black thread, but it really was made of three parts. One of these was a slender tube that ended in a hard, sharp point. The other two parts spread out and then came together in a shield. This shield protected the tube while Meg's muscles pushed it through bark and wood until it went into a burrow. There Meg laid a single egg. When it hatched, the larva would creep through the burrow until it found a horntail grub. The ichneumon-wasp larva would fasten itself to the young horntail. There the larva would stay and feed until it was ready to become a pupa.

There are many different kinds of ichneumon wasps. Some are as large as Meg but others are tiny, and their colors range from golden yellow to brown or shiny black. Most kinds, however, are alike in one way, for their larvae feed on caterpillars or grubs that are still alive. One common brown ichneumon wasp lays its eggs on the caterpillars of moths such as promethea (page 23). When one of these caterpillars turns into a pupa, the ichneumon-wasp larva spins a cocoon inside it and becomes a pupa, too. The promethea always dies, but the other insect keeps on changing inside its cocoon and case. When spring comes, it becomes a full-grown ichneumon wasp and crawls out of the cocoon.

.   .   .   .

There are hundreds of thousands of kinds of insects, and most of them are small. We expect their eggs to be small, too—and that is what most of them are. A moth whose wings are six inches wide starts out as a caterpillar not much longer than this dash —. The caterpillar comes from an egg that is only twice as wide as a pinhead. Many other insect eggs are so tiny that a pinhead would hold dozens of them.

Some birds lay only three or four eggs, and others lay a single large one. But insects, whose eggs are tiny, can lay many of them. A promethea moth may put thirty eggs on a single leaf, and she goes from leaf to leaf until her eggs number two or three hundred. A house fly produces five hundred or more, while a queen honey bee may lay two to three thousand eggs a day for several weeks. But the champion egg layers of the insect world are queen termites, or "white ants." A termite queen can lay an egg every second of every minute while three and a half to five weeks go by. If you figure it out you will find that she lays two to three *million* eggs!

Although insect eggs are small, they have many shapes. Large moths lay eggs that are smooth and flattened, like biscuits before

29

they are baked. Some butterfly eggs are pointed or are covered with ridges. Other eggs look like vases, buds, beads, or flowers. The eggs of lacewing flies are just plain egg-shaped, but each one hangs at the end of a slender thread. Mayfly eggs are balls with two long threads that wrap around sticks and plants floating at the surface of streams and ponds. The eggs also float till they hatch into nymphs that go to the bottom.

The mother ichneumon fly has a special egg-layer, whose scientific name is ovipositor (ó vi poz′ i ter). We have seen how Meg used her ovipositor to put her eggs in tunnels where horn-tail larvae were living.

Other insects have different egg-layers and use them in different ways. "Short-horned" grasshoppers, like the one shown on page 59, have four sharp points on the abdomen. The female drills a hole in the ground with these points and lays her eggs in it. Long-horned grasshoppers (page 31) have swordlike egg-layers that can be pushed into the ground. The cicada, which is also called harvest fly or locust, has a little saw at the tip of her

Insect eggs have many different shapes.

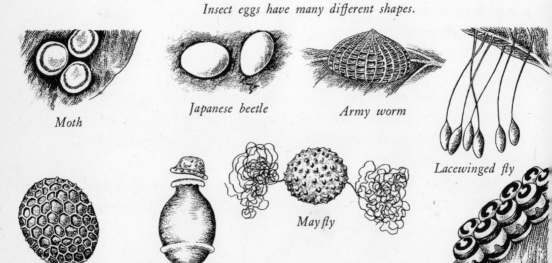

Moth

Japanese beetle

Army worm

Lacewinged fly

Leaf miner

Stone fly

Mayfly

Harlequin bug

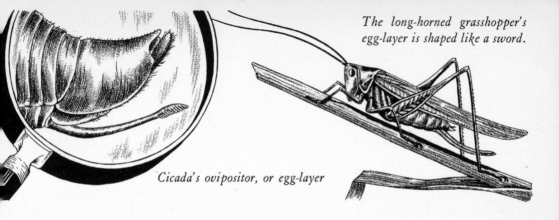

The long-horned grasshopper's egg-layer is shaped like a sword.

Cicada's ovipositor, or egg-layer

abdomen. The saw cuts slits in tender twigs, and the insect lays her eggs in holes at the bottom of each slit.

Many wasps and bees have egg-layers that also are stings. These insects can push their stings into other creatures and then squirt poison into their bodies. The poison kills small creatures or makes them unable to move, and it hurts others very badly, as you know if you have been stung by a wasp or bee. Most bees that sting do not lay eggs. They also die after stinging, for they cannot pull their stings out after they have used them. But many wasps can sting at one time and lay eggs at another, just by using different muscles. Some of these wasps sting other insects so they cannot move and then lay eggs on them. Then, when the larvae hatch, they eat the creatures which their mother has stung.

·   ·   ·   ·

Meg did two important things when she laid each egg in a horntail's burrow. First, she made sure that her little one would have food. Second, she put the egg where other creatures could not find it and eat it.

Many other insects do both these things but some do only one. When a grasshopper lays its eggs in the ground, it hides them

31

The praying mantis lays its eggs in froth that hardens into a case.

A male water bug with eggs on its back.

where they can lie safely until next summer comes. But the nymphs cannot find food in the ground, and must crawl out before they can eat. Cicada eggs are hidden under bark, but the little ones have to dig into the ground, where they suck juice from roots. The mother mantis lays her eggs on weeds or twigs and covers them with froth that soon hardens. It keeps the eggs from harm, but when the nymphs hatch they have to go out and catch their own breakfasts. Their mother has no way of storing up food for them.

Other insects do not hide their eggs, but put them where the young ones can find food. Aster's mother did that when she laid her eggs on parsnip leaves. Other butterflies and moths choose different plants, for their young ones do not like parsnips. Mother boll weevils, which are small beetles, chew holes in the buds, or "squares," of cotton. One egg is put into every hole, and the grub stays there eating and growing until it becomes a beetle.

Most insects take no care of their eggs and pay no attention to their young ones. But many bees, wasps, and ants protect their eggs and feed their babies. Among some water bugs, the mother even fastens her eggs to the father's back. He carries the eggs about until they hatch. Then he swims around with his little ones, protecting them from fish and from hungry insects.

Aphids, which we often call plant lice, are little green insects that suck juice from leaves, stems, and twigs. When fall comes, aphids mate and the mother lays her eggs on plants. Next spring these eggs hatch into females—never into males. These females do not have to mate, and they do not lay their eggs. Instead, the eggs stay safely in the mother's abdomen. When the little ones hatch, we often say that they are "born." Actually, they come out of their mother's body as tiny insects that are able to suck their own food.

Aphids often become so common that hundreds and even thousands of them suck juice from a single plant. In the summer, every one of these aphids is a female who hides her eggs inside her body, where other creatures cannot find them and eat them. Can you think of any better way for an insect to take care of her eggs?

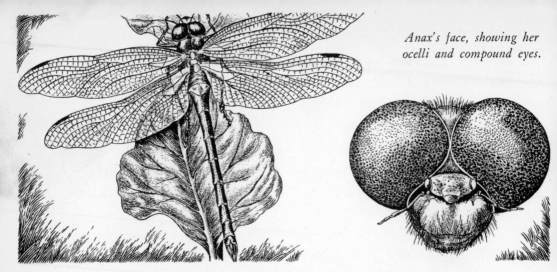

Anax, the green darner dragonfly, has two kinds of eyes.

Seeing and Other Senses

ANAX, a dragonfly, rested on the tip of a weed. Her four clear wings were spread out on both sides of her body, and they glistened in the sunshine. Her body glistened, too, for it was shiny green.

There are many kinds of dragonflies, and they belong to several families, or groups. Lib and her relatives (page 19) are called skimmers because they often fly very low over ponds and streams. Skimmers have broad abdomens, and most kinds have spots on their bodies as well as upon their wings. They also have chalky white patches that disappear when the dragonflies die.

Skimmers feed on small insects which also fly over streams and ponds. When a mother skimmer wants to lay eggs, she stops hunting and skims still closer to the water. Every few minutes she flies so low that her abdomen dips below the surface. As

34

she does this, eggs come out of her abdomen and are washed away. They soon sink to the bottom, where they lie until they hatch into nymphs that resemble Lib.

Dragonflies such as Anax are called green darners. They often fly far from water and hunt food high up in the air. Their abdomens are slender, and their bodies and wings never have chalky spots. Most of these insects also are shiny, though some kinds are red or brown instead of green.

When Anax and her relatives are ready to lay eggs, they alight on water plants and crawl down under the surface. Some species then cut slits in the stems and put their eggs into them. Others lay their eggs in the water and let them settle on the bottom. Nymphs that hatch from these eggs move about more often and walk faster than skimmer nymphs ever do.

.   .   .   .

It was past six o'clock when Anax perched upon the weed. She had been flying about to catch insects, but she still had a big appetite. When a swarm of flies came toward her, she left her perch and darted toward them. She held her six black legs so that her feet came together, forming a basket under her chin. The basket scooped up fly after fly as Anax flew to and fro. Hairs on her legs and feet kept the flies from getting away after they were caught.

When Anax caught good-sized insects, she sat on twigs or tall weeds to eat them. But these flies were almost as small as mosquitoes. The dragonfly could push them up to her mouth and chew them while she was catching more.

Just as Anax bit into one fly, a much larger creature zoomed toward her. It was a dark gray bird called the nighthawk, which also feeds upon insects. Its big mouth was wide open, ready to swallow Anax.

She saw the nighthawk just in time to dodge and dart toward the ground. The bird dodged too, but missed her. As it flew away, Anax hid in a bush. It was a fine place to keep away from danger and to spend the night. The big dragonfly went to sleep and did not wake up until morning came.

.   .   .   .

Anax saw both the flies and the nighthawk with two big eyes that covered most of her head. She also had two smaller eyes in front of the large ones, but these small eyes were not very good. Anax used them only to tell bright light from shade.

Silverfish and some other small insects have only these little eyes, which are called ocelli (o sell' i). They also are known as simple eyes because they are not made up of sections. If you could look at a simple eye through a microscope, you would find that it looks like a tiny cup. The cup is filled with clear, hard ma-

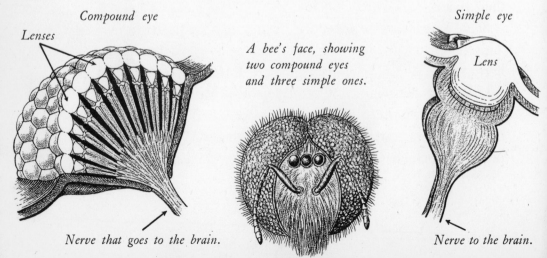

The parts of compound and simple eyes.

Compound eye

Lenses

*A bee's face, showing
two compound eyes
and three simple ones.*

Simple eye

Lens

Nerve that goes to the brain.

Nerve to the brain.

terial that forms a lens. The lens does not see shapes distinctly because it is shaped like a slightly flattened ball.

Large eyes are called compound because they are made up of sections covered by one clear coat. A thickened spot over each section forms a lens shaped like the one in your own eye. This sort of lens makes a much sharper "picture" than the lenses of ocelli can produce.

Some compound eyes have only a few sections, but others have hundreds or thousands of them. One eye of a big dragonfly, such as Anax, has 28,000 sections and lenses.

This does not mean that Anax sees every fly or tree or bird 28,000 times. Each eye-section looks at one bit of space. The next section looks at a bit of space near it, and so on. Nerves take all these sight messages to the brain, which fits them into one picture. Our brains do the same thing with messages that come from our two eyes.

The eyes of different insects fit the creatures' habits. Female fireflies, as we know, sit in the grass and flash their lights until the males come to them. The females have only 300 lenses in each eye and cannot see very well. But males, which must find the females, have 2,500 lenses and can see much better than their mates.

Some insects can see better and farther than we think they do. This is because they pay no attention to things that will not harm them, and to creatures that are far away. The insects' eyes look at these far-away creatures, but their brains are not affected. We do the same thing when we watch an automobile that is coming toward us but pay no attention to houses and people a block or two away.

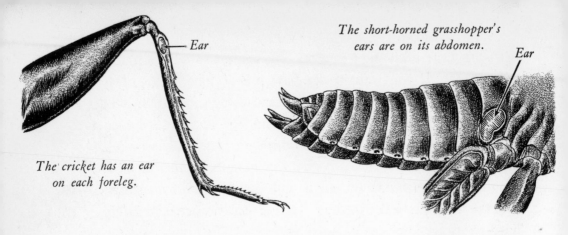

Ear

The short-horned grasshopper's ears are on its abdomen.

Ear

The cricket has an ear on each foreleg.

Insects that do not see very well are able to hear, taste, smell, and feel. Even creatures with good eyes may use these other senses to find food, discover mates, or tell when enemies are coming.

We human beings hear with two ears, one on each side of the head. But an insect's ears are different from ours, and they are found in different places. Grasshoppers with short "horns," or antennae, have ears that are thin ovals of skin on the abdomen, just behind the jumping legs. These ears hear the buzzing or clacking sounds made by other grasshoppers. Several beetles have ears on the thorax and abdomen, but male mosquitoes hear with their branched antennae.

Some moths also have ears on their abdomens. But the ears of long-horned grasshoppers, katydids, and crickets are located on their forelegs. We often say that these insects listen with their elbows.

Female mosquitoes hum by moving their wings very rapidly. The male hears this sound with tiny hairs on his bushy antennae, and flies to the nearest female. He can hear her when she is much too far away to be seen.

38

Insects taste with their mouths, but some also use their feet or antennae. If you want to see how this is done, drop a few grains of sand and sugar where flies are walking about. They will pay no attention to the sand, but when one of them steps on some sugar, he touches it carefully with his feet. They soon tell him it is good to eat, for he begins to scrape the grains with his tongue. He also softens the sugar with juice from his mouth, so that the food can be brushed up. That is much easier than eating hard scrapings.

Honeybees and wasps often taste with their antennae. A bee sometimes touches water with its antennae and then goes away. But if the water has sugar in it, the bee will take a drink. Its antennae can taste the difference between plain water and water that is sweet.

Butterflies use their eyes to find food, for they go to bright-colored flowers that contain nectar. But butterflies also smell with their antennae and taste with their feet. The insects will fly a long way to a tree where sap is running out of the bark. When they get there, they touch the sap with their feet before unrolling their tongues.

Silk moths smell with their antennae, for that is how they find their mates. Other moths also smell their food. Sphinx, or hummingbird, moths fly to sweet-smelling flowers at night, when their colors cannot be seen. Underwings fly long distances to mixtures of spoiled fruit and molasses which people who collect insects sometimes put on trees. Other moths also come to this bait, where collectors easily catch them.

Moths and butterflies use their sense of smell when they choose places to lay their eggs. The eggs could hatch on almost any-

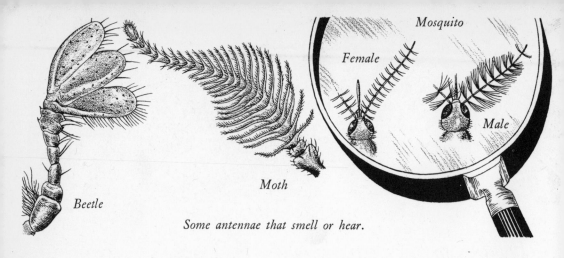

Some antennae that smell or hear.

thing, but the caterpillars must have special foods. Aster, for example, eats leaves of carrot plants and their relatives, but monarch caterpillars feed on milkweed. Scientists think that a mother butterfly or moth finds the right plant by smelling and then lays her eggs on it. Meg and other ichneumon wasps put their antennae against wood or stick them into burrows. In this way the wasps "smell out" the kinds of insects their own little ones can eat. If there is no smell at all, or a wrong one, the mothers do not lay their eggs.

We sometimes call antennae "feelers," and some insects do touch things with them. But most insects are also able to feel with their feet, with jointed structures on their heads and abdomens, or with hairs on different parts of their bodies. Many insects that see poorly can tell every movement of the plants on which they rest or feed, and they feel every vibration in the ground. These creatures can easily tell when enemies are coming. If these insects eat larvae or other full-grown insects, they can also tell when food is near.

40

*Digger loosened grains
of sand and soil.*

Foods and What Happens to Them

DIGGER flew over a pasture one bright summer morning. Her
wings moved so fast that they made a buzzing sound. Her
brownish-black body was more than an inch long. Bright yellow
bands ran around it, and a narrow waist separated her thorax
from her abdomen.

Digger was one of the insects known as hunting wasps. People
also called her a digger wasp, a cicada killer, and a solitary wasp.
The last of these names means that Digger lived alone, not in a
nest with her sisters and brothers. The other names tell us some
of the things she did.

Digger was looking for something as she flew about the pasture. She was looking for a dry slope where the soil was partly
sand. When she saw what she wanted she flew down to the
ground and began to dig.

The big wasp dug with her forelegs, which had spines like
the teeth of a rake. Digger raised her legs and brought them
down with a sweeping movement. As she did so, the "teeth"
loosened sand grains and pulled them under her body. Then she

41

pushed the sand grains behind her with another pair of feet. By raking and pushing she soon made a tunnel that went straight back into the bank.

Digger made her tunnel longer and longer, smoothing its sides as she went. When a pebble got in her way she took hold of it with her jaws. Next she pulled and tugged until the pebble came loose. After that she backed out of the tunnel, pushing loose soil and sand behind her. When the dirt spilled out of her door, she turned and dropped the pebble beside it. Then she hurried back into the tunnel and began to dig again.

When the tunnel was about 18 inches long, Digger scraped out a round room at the end. When that was done she backed out again and flew to a grove of trees where cicadas were singing.

A cicada (si kay′ duh) is a large insect with a broad, short head and wings that shine like glass. We often call cicadas locusts or harvest flies. They sing their loud, buzzing songs on hot summer days.

Two cicadas flew away as soon as Digger came near. Another cicada was so busy singing that it did not notice her. Digger knocked this insect from its perch and held onto it while it fell to the ground. Then she turned the cicada over and stung it on the under side of its thorax. The sting was not strong enough to kill. Instead, it paralyzed the cicada, or made it so it could not move. Many scientists think that paralyzed insects cannot even feel.

Digger stood over the cicada until it lay quite still. Then she took hold of it with her middle legs, one on each side of its body. She began to walk with the rest of her legs, dragging the cicada under her.

Instead of walking toward her burrow, Digger went to an oak tree. When she reached it, she climbed almost as high as a man's shoulder. Then she spread her wings and flew toward the sandy bank.

Digger could fly long distances when she did not have a load. But the cicada weighed more than she did. She was able to carry it for a while, but its weight made her come back to the ground. She had to climb a weed in order to fly again—and again she had to come back to the ground. In fact, Digger climbed and flew four different times before she reached her burrow.

Climbing and flying made the big wasp tired, but she did not rest. Instead, she dragged the cicada into the room, which we call a cell. There she laid an egg on the creature's thorax, near one of its middle legs. The egg would soon hatch into a larva that would feed upon the cicada for a week or two. At the end of that time the baby wasp would become a pupa.

When the egg was laid, Digger crawled out and closed the door of the cell with a thin wall of dirt. Two days later she dug

Digger carried the cicada to her burrow.

another cell, put a cicada in it, and laid another egg. She did this again and again, until she had dug five cells and brought home five cicadas for her little ones to eat.

. . . .

There are many kinds of hunting wasps, and their young ones eat different foods. Some mother wasps sting grasshoppers, but others store up caterpillars for their hungry larvae. A few catch other kinds of wasps. The largest hunting wasp stings the big, hairy spiders known as tarantulas. Tarantula hawks, as these wasps are called, have blue-black bodies and orange wings, and grow as much as two inches long.

All these hunting wasps are solitary, and they all dig burrows. But the solitary wasps called mud daubers never burrow, even though they hunt.

Mud daubers (page 72) are much smaller than Digger, and their slender waists are much longer than hers. They build tube-shaped nests out of mud and fill them with small spiders. Some kinds put two or three tubes side by side, but others build as many as twenty and stand them on end.

. . . .

If you look at an insect's mouth, you can tell how it eats. Caterpillars have biting jaws that nip off pieces of leaf and chew them until they are soft. So do grasshoppers and many beetles, but other insects use their jaws to catch and eat small animals. Some ants do more than that, for they crawl over large creatures and eat them. An "army" of these savage ants can kill and devour a pig, a deer, or even a scaly snake.

Jaws are not the only things used to capture food. Every baby

44

dragonfly, or nymph, has a hinged lower lip that shoots out and catches such things as mosquito wrigglers. The mantis has two spiny forelegs that seize other insects and hold them while they are being eaten. The giant water bug also has grasping forelegs, though the bug sucks food from its victims instead of chewing them.

Many insects suck their food from other animals or from plants. A butterfly or moth does this with its "tongue," which scientists call a proboscis (pro boss' iss). The tongue is a slender tube which can be rolled up close to the head. It can be unrolled to suck sweet juice, called nectar, from flowers. Butterflies also suck sap that oozes out of trees, or drink water from puddles.

A mosquito's sucking tube is much shorter than a butterfly's tongue. It also is made from different parts of the mouth, and the female mosquito uses it to suck blood, not juice. Around the

The praying mantis holds its food between spiny feet. The cicada sucks food through a short tube, but the butterfly's tube-shaped tongue is very long and can be rolled up under its head.

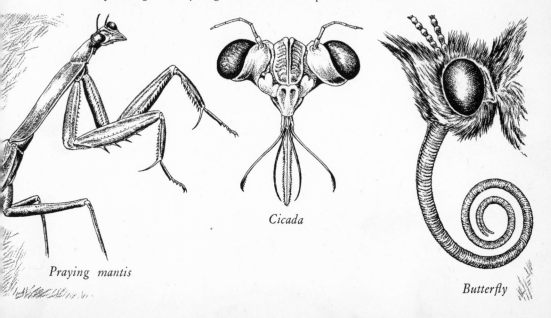

Cicada

Praying mantis

Butterfly

Esophagus

Crop *Gizzard*

Stomach

Intestine

Pharynx

Mouth

Seven parts of the tube in which an insect digests its food.

tube she has daggers that cut a hole in the skin of beasts or human beings, so the insect can feed on blood. Male mosquitoes have different appetites, for they suck juice from plants.

Most bugs also feed on plant juice, but some suck food from the bodies of other insects, tadpoles, or fish. The honeybee has a tube and something that looks like a tongue, which laps up nectar from flowers. But the house-fly's "tongue" is its lower lip, which forms a tube that spreads out at the bottom and is covered with hard, rough ridges. They scrape tiny bits from dry food or brush up foods that are moist. Actually, the fly can moisten dry food as fast as bits are scraped loose. The moistened food is then brushed into the insect's mouth.

. . . .

An insect uses its food to live and to build up its body. But before food can be used, it has to be digested. Food is digested in an irregular tube that starts in the insect's head and goes to the tip of its abdomen. The tube is divided into parts that have different shapes and different names, and do different work.

46

Let's imagine we can look inside an insect and find out what these parts are. The first one is the pharynx (făr′ inks), and it seems to be the back of the mouth. In some insects the pharynx is small, but in sucking insects it is large and works like a pump. It sucks nectar from flowers and juice from stems, and it draws blood from skin. When a mosquito "bites" it pumps blood into its mouth by swelling and then squeezing its pharynx.

The esophagus (ee sof′ a guss) is part of the tube which might be called the throat. It is narrow where it goes through the joint just back of the head, but it is larger in the thorax. In many insects the esophagus becomes a pocket or pouch which is called the crop. The crop holds extra food until it can be digested.

Some insects have no gizzard, but many others do. It is a pouch that is covered with strong muscles and is lined with toothlike bumps or ridges. When the muscles move, these "teeth" grind solid food until it is almost like liquid. A bird's gizzard works the same way, except that it uses pebbles instead of ridges and bumps.

An insect's stomach may be larger and thicker than the crop, or it may be smaller. The stomach is the place where ground-up food is digested, or changed so it can go out into the insect's watery blood. The insect uses digested food in growing, in moving about, and doing all the other things that are parts of living. Food material that cannot be digested goes into the intestine. There it stays until muscles push it out of the insect's body.

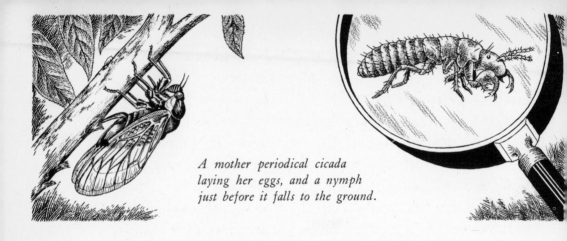

*A mother periodical cicada
laying her eggs, and a nymph
just before it falls to the ground.*

Insects in the Ground

ONE June day a mother cicada alighted on a willow tree. She was a big, blackish insect with a broad, blunt head and red eyes. Her shiny wings folded back but did not overlap. They sloped over her back like the two sides of a low roof.

The cicada sat still for a while and then walked along a twig. Soon she stopped and pressed her curved egg-layer against the twig. The egg-layer was almost as sharp as a knife, and the cicada used it to cut a slit on the under side of the twig. Next she dug two small holes, or cells, with a thin wall of wood between them.

When the cells were dug, the mother cicada laid her eggs in them. She put two rows of eggs in each cell, with six or seven eggs in each row. Then the cicada flew away to dig more cells and lay more eggs in another twig.

Several weeks went by before the eggs began to hatch. The little ones, which were nymphs, first crawled out of the shells. Then they wriggled until they split some very thin membranes

48

that covered their tiny bodies. After that the nymphs crept out through the slit in the bark and sat on the twig.

Tib was the first nymph to hatch, and the first one to go outdoors. He soon started to walk along the twig, but its bark was so smooth that his feet lost their hold. Tib tried to catch himself, but missed. In a moment he tumbled all the way down to the ground.

The fall did not hurt Tib, for his body was not heavy enough to strike the ground with a *bump!* Besides, all cicada nymphs have to get to the ground a few minutes after they hatch. Most of them fall out of trees, but some are blown off by wind.

As soon as Tib reached the ground, he hid under a very young tree. The moment he found a crack in the ground, he began to dig. Down he went until he was among the roots of the little tree. Then he stopped to rest.

After Tib had rested for several hours, he began to feel hungry. He took hold of a root with his feet and pushed his sharp beak into it. Then he began to suck juice, or sap. Like grownup cicadas, Tib had a mouth with a sucking tube and could not eat solid food.

After Tib had sucked two or three meals, he felt strong enough to make a home. He dug it in the ground, around the juicy root.

When ants or yellowjackets dig underground homes, they loosen grains of dirt and carry them to the surface. But Tib used an easier method. First he moistened dirt around the root with water which he got from sap. Then he pushed the moist dirt away from the root. Soon he had a little room with tightly packed walls. When the moisture dried, the room's walls also became hard. They had only two openings, where the root came in and where it went out.

Tib sucked sap in his room all through the summer and autumn. When winter came and the ground grew cold, he went to sleep, or hibernated. In the spring he woke up and sucked sap again. Sometimes he also cleaned his forelegs by rubbing them against his face, which was covered with bristles.

When Tib was about one year old, he molted and became larger. He made his room larger, too, by wetting the walls and pushing against them. The longer and harder he pushed, the bigger his room became.

That summer was a very dry one, and the little tree died. Tib waited three or four days, as if he expected the tree to come to life again. Then he dug through the ground till he came to the roots of a weed. Since they were alive and juicy, he settled down beside them and dug another room.

Some cicadas live in the ground one or two years and then become adults. One of these cicadas is often called the harvest fly. It is a black-and-green insect that measures about an inch

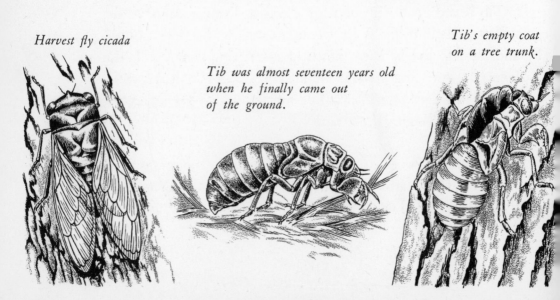

Harvest fly cicada

Tib was almost seventeen years old when he finally came out of the ground.

Tib's empty coat on a tree trunk.

and a quarter in length. It comes out of the ground in July or August, and sings loudly on hot days.

Tib belonged to another kind, or species, which never becomes more than one and one half inches long. It has red markings on its under side, and the adult insects fly about during May and June. Their proper name is periodical cicada, but they are often called seventeen-year locusts. Many of them do take seventeen years to grow up, but others take only thirteen years.

Tib was a periodical cicada that lived seventeen years, and he spent all but the last six weeks in the ground. During those years he molted six times and made three or four rooms.

Tib had to get out of the ground before he could become an adult insect. When the time came to make this change, he stood at one end of his room and began to push his way upward. When he came near the surface, he stopped and waited till evening. Then he pushed through the last bit of soil and crawled out. Many other cicadas were doing this, too. About three hundred of them were Tib's brothers and sisters. All of them had come from the eggs his mother laid in willow twigs.

Tib rested on the ground for a while. Then he went to the willow and climbed a short way up the trunk. There he stopped and held to the bark so tightly that nothing could pull him loose. After resting a while he bent till his coat split down the back. Tib crawled out as an adult cicada, and left his old, empty nymph coat clinging to the bark.

.   .   .   .

Many other insects spend their early lives in the ground. All June "bugs" (they really are beetles) are ground-dwellers while they are young. The larvae, which we often call white grubs, have brown heads, white bodies that curl up, and long, hairy legs. The grubs chew roots instead of sucking sap, and they often kill large numbers of plants.

One of the strangest insects whose young ones live in the ground is the carrion, or burying, beetle. Carrion is some dead and decaying animal. When a pair of carrion beetles find a dead mouse or small bird on the ground, they crawl part way under it and start to dig a hole. As soon as the hole becomes fairly large, the beetles pull the dead creature into the hollow. Then they go back to digging again. They keep on working until the mouse or bird is completely underground and is covered by dirt that falls on top of it.

At last we find out why the beetles do all this hard work. They dig a hole near the carrion and mate there. Next the female digs a tunnel to the buried carrion. She lays her eggs in the tunnel and stays near them, eating some of the dead meat for food. When the larvae hatch, their mother feeds them with drops of

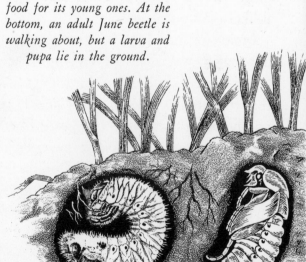

The carrion beetle (left) buries food for its young ones. At the bottom, an adult June beetle is walking about, but a larva and pupa lie in the ground.

*Mole cricket and
one of its digging feet.*

meat which she has partly digested. It makes the larvae strong
enough to feed themselves.

Most insect children never see their parents, but young carrion
beetles live with their mother for several days. Then they burrow
into soil beside their buried food and turn into pupae. When the
pupae become full-grown beetles, they dig *upward* to the surface of the ground.

．　　　．　　　．　　　．

Another strange burrowing insect is the mole cricket. It digs
rooms and tunnels in damp soil, and eats larvae, worms and
other small creatures which it finds in the ground while it is digging. The cricket also cuts roots and chews pieces from them if
it likes their taste.

Moles are furry little beasts whose forefeet are very large and
are shaped just right for digging. The mole cricket also has
broad forefeet, with points that dig into the dirt and sharp ridges
that cut through roots. A thick shield covers the insect's thorax
and helps push dirt out of the way. The hind legs are built for
pushing, not hopping. When the cricket wants to travel at the
surface, it crawls or spreads its hind wings and flies. The hind
wings are long and wide, but the forewings are much too small
to carry the mole cricket's body.

The water boatman swims with oarlike feet or walks under water.

Life Under Water

CORIX, a water boatman, dived to the bottom of his pond. There he reached out and hooked one of his claws into the stem of a plant called the arrowhead. This kept him from bobbing up to the surface, for his body was light enough to float.

Water boatmen are medium-sized insects that are shaped like shallow rowboats. Their colors are a mixture of gray and black, and their coats are covered with velvety hairs. They have thin wings and are able to fly, but they spend most of their time in ponds, shallow lakes, and streams.

The water boatman has three kinds of legs, and it uses them in different ways. The long hind legs are shaped like oars. The insect uses them as we use oars, except it generally rows under water, not at the surface.

The middle legs are very long, and the feet end in hooks. A water boatman can walk on the bottom with these legs, or can hold onto plants with them.

54

The first pair of legs is short, and their edges look like tiny rakes. The insect uses these legs to gather food.

Corix was looking for food when he dived and took hold of the arrowhead stem. He did not try to eat the stem, for it was much too large. Instead, Corix leaned sideways and began to scrape scum from the bottom of the pond. The scum looked like sticky green mud, but it really was full of tiny plants called algae (al′ jee). Although Corix did not have a name for algae, they were his favorite food.

Some of the algae were soft, but the kinds Corix liked best had shells. He sucked the juicy "flesh" that filled them and then let the shells fall to the bottom. He had to suck hundreds of algae to get one good-sized meal.

Corix stayed at the bottom of the pond so long that he had to breathe. Fish breathe the gas called oxygen from water, and so do tadpoles, which are young toads or frogs. But Corix was an insect, and he had to get oxygen from air. How could he do that while he was diving or eating algae in the pond?

Corix could not get air under water. But he could get oxygen if he took a supply of air with him when he dived. And that was just what he did, right in the middle of his meal. First he pulled his hooked claws from the arrowhead stem and bobbed up to the surface. There he floated while bubbles of air fastened themselves to velvety hairs that covered his body. When Corix dived, this air stayed on the hairs. It gave him all the oxygen he needed while he finished his meal.

Corix is one of the insects which scientists mean when they use the name "bug." Many bugs have broad, flat bodies and wings that overlap when they are folded. Some kinds produce

Box-elder bug

Spiny tree bug

Chinch bug

Three true bugs that live on land and suck juice from plants.

unpleasant tastes and odors which keep them from being eaten by birds and other creatures. All bugs have mouths built for sucking, not for biting or chewing. No real bug could ever cut its food into tiny pieces or grind wood into paper, as many wasps do.

Squash bugs, chinch bugs, and plant bugs live on land, and so do many others. But water boatmen are not the only ones that make their homes in lakes, ponds, and streams. The back swimmer, for example, is a slender bug that resembles Corix except that it swims on its back. Its oar-shaped hind legs are long, and they send its narrow body through the water very swiftly. Back swimmers feed upon smaller insects and other creatures which they catch and sting. Hairs on the abdomen and thorax hold bubbles of air which the insects need for breathing.

Do you remember the broad brown water bug whose mate lays her eggs on his back? These insects are water-dwellers, too, though they can crawl out and fly when they want to go from one stream to another. They generally fly at night, and they often go to electric lights. There the bugs often fly around and around until their wings are damaged and they die.

Giant water bugs are still larger, for they are two to three inches long. They also fly around electric lights when they go on land. In the water, they hide under sticks or stones, darting out to catch insects, worms, tadpoles, and even small fish. These bugs have sharp sucking tubes that can go through a human being's skin. If you catch a giant water bug, don't try to cover it with your hand.

The water strider is a bug whose wings have almost disappeared. As you can guess from its name, it is able to stride, or walk and run, on water. Some kinds can also dive, but others drown if they cannot get back to the surface very quickly.

You can tell water striders by their slender bodies, which are about half an inch long. The first pair of legs is short and is used to catch food. The middle legs and hind legs are very long, and the feet are covered with very fine hairs. They rest on the topmost part of the water, which is called the surface layer. This layer is just tough enough to keep the insects from sinking, for they do not weigh much. They seem to skate over the water, and

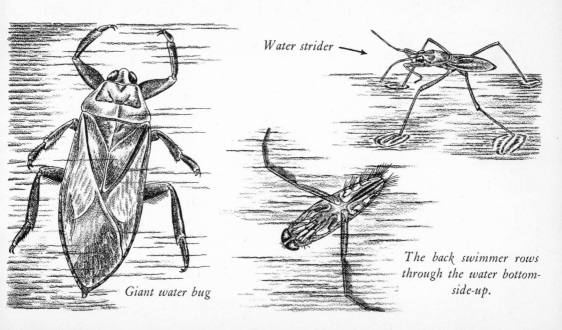

Water strider →

Giant water bug

The back swimmer rows through the water bottom-side-up.

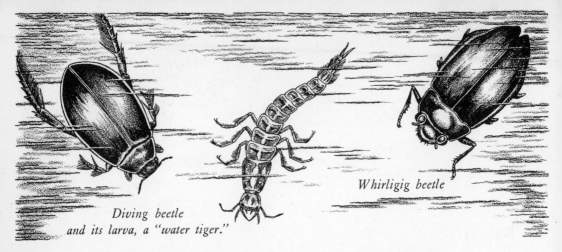

Diving beetle
and its larva, a "water tiger."

Whirligig beetle

Two kinds of beetles that spend most of their lives in the water.

they sometimes jump into the air to catch other insects for food.

The commonest water insects are bugs, but beetles of several kinds also live in ponds and streams. Those we know best are the diving beetles. You can tell them from bugs by their hard forewings, which form a smooth shield over the back. Diving beetles have big appetites, and they eat other insects, tadpoles, or even small fish. Larval diving beetles are called water tigers. They have wormlike bodies, six strong legs, and hollow jaws with openings near the end. The "tiger" catches insects and other small creatures, and sucks their blood through these openings in its jaws.

Water scavengers look like diving beetles but grow much larger, for one common species becomes three and a half inches long. Their larvae also are "water tigers" that catch living creatures, though adult scavenger beetles generally eat dead things. But grown-up whirligig beetles are hunters. You can tell them by their habit of swimming in zigzags and circles at the surface. They dive when something alarms them.

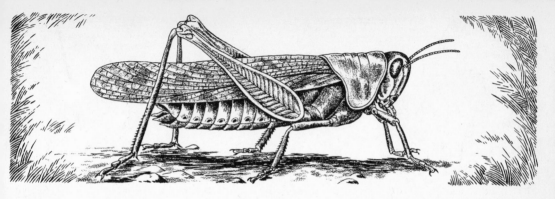

Spiracles show on the abdomen of this "short-horned" grasshopper.

Breathing on Land and in Water

LONG-LEGS, a grasshopper, was tired. Boys who wanted bait for fishing had been chasing him. First they came so close that he had to jump, and then they ran after him. They did this again and again, even when Long-legs spread his black-and-red wings and flew after he jumped. But at last the boys gave up and went away. Long-legs sat on the ground to rest and catch his breath.

When we human beings breathe, air comes into our nostrils and fills our lungs. The lungs, of course, are in our chests. You know how your own chest becomes larger every time you take a deep breath.

Long-legs breathed in a different way, for he had no lungs or nostrils. He got air through rows of openings called spiracles (spire´ a klz) on both sides of his body. Little bags, or sacs, in his abdomen kept the air moving. When the sacs became larger, or expanded, they pumped air in through the spiracles. When the sacs grew small, or contracted, they pushed the air out of the spiracles again.

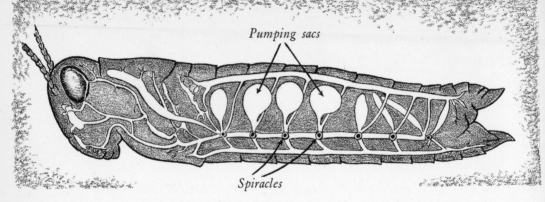

Spiracles, pumping sacs, and branching tubes in a grasshopper's body.

After air came into the spiracles, it flowed through breathing tubes. Some of the tubes ran lengthwise, especially through the abdomen. Other tubes divided, or branched, in all directions. They went into every part of the grasshopper's body, from his eyes and antennae to his feet and the tip of his abdomen.

The walls of these branched tubes were so thin that two things could happen. First, oxygen from the air went through them and spread into all the parts of the grasshopper's body. As the oxygen spread, it combined with food. This process produced energy which moved Long-legs' muscles and kept him alive. Long-legs used a great deal of energy when he was jumping and flying. He needed energy when he sat still, too. He used it to listen, smell, look about, and pump air through his spiracles.

The second thing that happened was almost as important as producing energy. When oxygen combined with food, it produced another gas known as carbon dioxide (di ox´ ide). Long-legs could not use carbon dioxide, and it could not be kept in his body. It went into his breathing tubes instead, and mixed with the air that was flowing through them. When the air went out of Long-legs' spiracles, it took the useless carbon dioxide along.

60

That is just what happens when air is "breathed out," or exhaled, from our lungs.

. . . .

Some insects have no sacs that pump air into their bodies and then force it out. But all grown-up insects that live on land breathe with spiracles and tubes. So do land-dwelling nymphs and larvae. If you look at almost any large, bare-skinned caterpillar, you will see its spiracles in the center of oval dots. Spiracles also show plainly on the sides of chrysalids and pupae. They are easy to examine there, since the insects cannot move about.

Most adult water insects breathe as do their relatives that live on land. Of course, most water insects take air with them when they dive. Those that stay under water very long also breathe the same air several times. Between breathings, carbon dioxide goes out into the water, purifying the air.

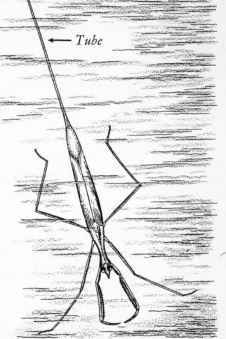

The water scorpion (right) gets air through a long breathing tube, but the mosquito larva and pupae have short tubes. The larva also uses gills.

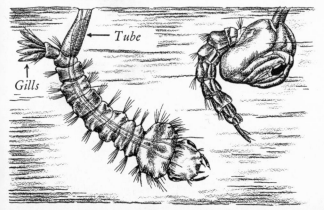

Water scorpions breathe in a different way, but they are not scorpions. They are slender bugs with four long, thin legs and two thick ones that capture other insects. The so-called scorpions often rest in water with their heads downward and their tails reaching up to the surface. Actually, each "tail" is a hollow tube, or siphon (sy′fun), that takes air down to spiracles at the end of the abdomen. This allows the water scorpion to breathe without bothering to carry bubbles of air under water.

The mosquito larva has a siphon, too, but it is thick and not very long. It sticks out near the end of the abdomen, making the larva look as if he had a forked tail. This siphon disappears when the larva turns into a pupa and two new, short siphons grow out from the thorax. They are shown on page 61.

If you look at a larval mosquito through a microscope, you will see four little leaves on the second fork of his tail. These leaves really are gills that breathe oxygen from water. The gill walls are so thin that oxygen goes through them, though water does not.

Young tadpoles and fish have gills right behind their heads. Insect gills grow farther back, upon the abdomen. A young may-

Spiracles on two moth pupae and a caterpillar.

Spotted sphinx, or "tomato worm."

Cecropia moth

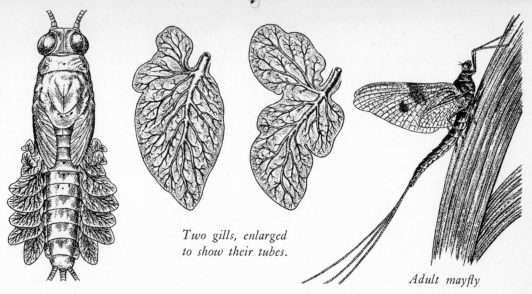

*Two gills, enlarged
to show their tubes.*

Adult mayfly

*Young mayflies live under water and breathe with
gills on their abdomens.*

fly's gills look like thin leaves, with "veins" that really are branched breathing tubes. Oxygen goes into these tubes and then flows through the body, while carbon dioxide comes out. A young dragonfly's gills work this way, too, but they are in a hollow, or chamber, inside the abdomen. We already know how the nymph pumps water into this chamber and then forces it out again. If the water moves slowly, the insect breathes. But when the water comes out in a sudden jet, it drives the nymph through the water like a tiny torpedo.

The simplest method of breathing under water is used by a few little larvae that have very thin skins. They soak up, or absorb, oxygen and let carbon dioxide go out. Such insects do not even need breathing tubes to take the oxygen through their bodies after it comes into their skins.

63

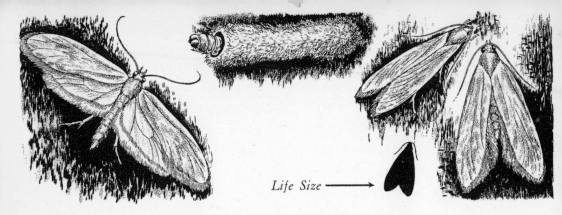

Life Size ⟶

The clothes moth is a common insect that lives in houses.
These pictures are enlarged.

Tiny and Other House-dwellers

TINY, the clothes-moth larva, hatched on an autumn morning. He nipped a hole in the eggshell that covered him and then wriggled out.

Tiny's mother had laid the egg only five days before. It was smooth and white and very small—about one-tenth as big as a pinhead. When Tiny hatched he was only one-sixteenth of an inch long, or not quite half as long as the dash between the words "small" and "about."

Moths that live outdoors lay their eggs in the spring or summer, when the weather is warm. These moths also fasten their eggs to plants which the larvae can eat.

Clothes moths can do things differently because they live in houses. The house in which Tiny's mother lived was heated by a furnace during autumn, winter, and early spring. The mother moth was able to lay eggs whenever she felt like it, and her little ones were never harmed by cold weather.

Young clothes moths do not feed on leaves, as do most larvae that live outdoors. Clothes-moth larvae like wool, fur, feathers, and rough leather. When Tiny's mother was ready to lay her eggs, she went into a dark closet. There she fastened almost a hundred eggs to an old woolen coat and two or three sweaters. Children wore the sweaters outdoors next day, and the eggs on them were destroyed. But no one wanted to wear the old coat, so the eggs on it were not harmed.

Tiny hatched from one of those eggs. When he crawled from the eggshell he started to eat, nipping bits of wool and chewing them until they were soft. Next he covered his dull white body with a tube-shaped case which he made from tiny bits of wool that were held together by silk. When Tiny lay in the case no one could see him, for he seemed to be part of the coat. Even when he crawled out far enough so he could eat, the case hid most of his body. No one who glanced at the coat could tell that Tiny was feeding on it.

Tiny ate so much that he soon had to molt. When he molted he grew larger and his woolen case became too small. He made it wider by cutting a slit down one side. Then he nipped off many more pieces of wool and pasted them into the slit. He also made the tube longer by pasting bits of wool at one end.

At first Tiny only made the cloth thin as he bit off pieces of wool. Then the thin place became a hole, and the hole grew so large that Tiny could not reach out and get food. He had to crawl a short distance away in order to eat again. He took his case with him when he moved.

If Tiny had hatched in the summer, he might have grown fast enough to become a pupa when he was six weeks old. But as autumn turned into winter, he did not grow so fast. Christmas and New Year's Day came before he stopped eating. Instead of becoming a pupa, he dropped to the floor of the closet, taking his case with him. Soon he crawled into a crack between two boards, and there he went to sleep.

Tiny slept for weeks and weeks, until spring arrived. Then he woke up and changed into a pupa without leaving his woolen case. The pupa was white at first but changed to brown, and then its coat split down the back. Out came Tiny as a small, wet moth who sat still while his wings spread out and grew stiff, and while the scales that covered them dried. The scales were such a pale, brownish buff that they looked silvery. When Tiny stretched his wings as wide as he could, they measured only half an inch from one tip to the other.

Although Tiny was very small, he had branched antennae like those of Prom and other big silk moths. He resembled Prom in another way, too, for he did not eat. When night came, he fluttered about the house until he met a female clothes moth and became her mate. Tiny died a few hours after mating, but the mother moth lived long enough to lay more than eighty eggs. She put them on clothing and in a closet like the one where Tiny had hatched and grown up.

There are several kinds of clothes moths, but two are specially common. Tiny belonged to the kind called the case-bearing clothes moth because the larva builds a woolen case and "bears," or drags, it around. The other kind is known as the webbing clothes moth. Its larvae never live in cases, but they spin threads of silk as they crawl about and feed. If the larvae are common, their threads of silk crisscross each other like webs. These webs are easier to see than Tiny's woolen case. Both species like darkness when they grow up, as well as they do when they are larvae. No clothes moth will fly toward a bright light, as other moths often do.

Clothes moths must have lived outdoors at one time, before people began to build homes. How did the moths change their habits, and turn into house-dwellers?

No one *knows* the answer to that question, but scientists have a theory that tells what probably happened. At first, says this theory, the insects that are now clothes moths lived in dens where wild animals slept. In these dark, damp places, the moth larvae ate hair that had rubbed off the animals' bodies.

As time went by, human beings began to kill animals and live in their caves. This was fine for the larvae, which could feed upon fur that was used for bedding or clothing. When people

These insects now make their homes in houses and other buildings.

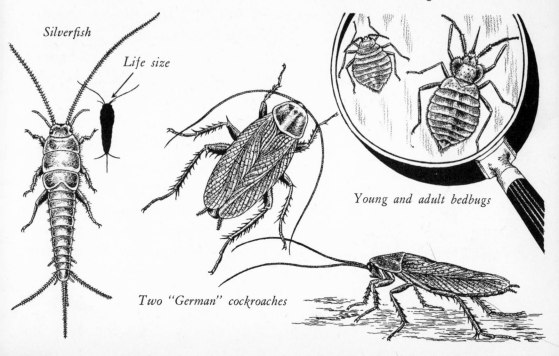

Silverfish

Life size

Young and adult bedbugs

Two "German" cockroaches

began to build huts, clothes moths moved into them, too. The moths moved again when houses were built instead of huts, and when people began to live in apartments. Our modern homes, which are heated all winter, are just as good for clothes moths as they are for us. The insects have become such perfect house-dwellers that they cannot live anywhere else.

. . . .

Clothes moths are not the only insects that have learned to live in houses. Silverfish and firebrats are house-dwellers. So are booklice, bedbugs, and broad-winged cockroaches.

Silverfish and firebrats are old-fashioned insects that have never developed wings. Their legs are short, their antennae are long, and three bristles grow at the end of the abdomen. Their metamorphosis is so incomplete that they hardly seem to have one. They neither change shape as they grow up nor develop new parts such as wings. All they do is become larger and shed their coats several times.

Both silverfish and firebrats like food that is mostly starch. They nibble at crumbs in kitchens and pantries, or in restaurants. They also chew at starched clothing and curtains, scrape paste from the covers of books, and eat the starchy surface that makes paper glossy. Rayon clothing is eaten, too, for it seems to taste as good as starch. In warm damp places, where these insects are common, they do a great deal of harm.

Cockroaches are not so old-fashioned as silverfish, for they have developed wings. Still, these insects were common during the Coal Age, a quarter of a billion years ago. This means that they are much older than beetles, bees, and moths.

Ancient cockroaches lived outdoors, for there were no buildings. Modern cockroaches can live outdoors, too, but they find better homes in greenhouses, grocery stores, bakeries, houses, and apartments. Cockroaches eat almost anything, and have big appetites. They also scatter filth and germs when they run or hide in dirty places and then walk over dishes or food.

Some cockroaches are small and are yellowish brown, but others are big and dark. You can tell most kinds by their flattened bodies and thin, broad wings, which fold over their backs. The antennae generally are long, and the legs are spiny. The eggs are put into a capsule, which the mother often carries around till they are almost ready to hatch. If you find an insect with something blunt at the end of its abdomen, you can be almost sure that you have a mother cockroach.

Some bedbugs live outdoors, but the commonest kind makes its home in hotels, houses, chicken houses, and barns. It is a flat-bodied, almost wingless little insect that hides in mattresses, cracks, and other dark places during the day. At night it comes out to bite human beings or other creatures and suck their warm blood. When the bedbug bites it puts poison into the skin, and this causes swelling, itching, or burning. Bedbug bites sometimes hurt for a week or more.

This cockroach lived during the Coal Age, many millions of years ago. Its coat is now in a slab of rock.

A paper wasp worker. At the right,
Pol is resting on her nest.

Insects That Live Together

POL, a young wasp, was sleeping in a hollow tree. She stayed there, without moving, from late autumn until May.

Pol was much smaller than Digger, but she plainly was a wasp. Her head had big eyes and two strong jaws, and her four wings folded flat against her back. A short, slender "waist" separated her abdomen from her thorax.

Digger lived alone, as do long-waisted wasps that build nests of mud. But Pol was one of the wasps that make nests of paper. Paper wasps live in groups, or colonies, that contain dozens or even hundreds of insects. All may be sisters—and sometimes brothers—or they may be the children of two or three mothers that build a single nest.

We say that insects living in colonies are "social." All paper wasps and many bees are social insects, and so are ants, termites, and some kinds of beetles.

Beetle colonies contain only the father, the mother, and a few young ones. But most social insects live in such large groups that they divide their work. Eggs are laid by special females, called queens, which mate with the males. Other females do most of the work, such as building nests, finding food, and taking care of the young ones. Some workers even become soldiers which fight other insects that attack the colony.

Pol was a young paper wasp queen. She had hatched and grown up the summer before, and had mated when autumn began. Then she hid in a hollow tree and slept until spring.

When Pol woke up, she crawled out of the tree and sat in the sunshine until her body was warm. Then she began to hunt for a place to build her nest. She flew around and around a house and a barn, and she looked in several trees. At last she found a spot that pleased her, under the eaves of a garage.

After choosing her nesting place, Pol flew to an old, weather-beaten post. There she scraped off bits of wood with her jaws, and chewed the bits into pulp. When the pulp was spread out it would dry into tough gray paper.

Pol chewed until her mouth was full, and then she went to the garage. There she pressed the pulp against a board, so tightly that it could not come loose. All day long she went to and fro, bringing pulp which she arranged in a stem that hung downward. Next she built a cup-shaped cell, which also hung upside down. Finally she laid an egg, which she fastened to the cell with glue.

This work took most of three days. Pol rested on the fourth day, but then she began to build more cells and put more eggs in them. In two weeks she built eleven cells. They formed a nest like a honeycomb of paper that hung from the stem.

As Pol built more cells and laid more eggs, her first eggs began to hatch. Each baby wasp was a grayish-white larva that hung with its head downward and its mouth near the opening of its cell. The larva's first meal was a drop of sweet nectar which its mother brought from flowers. After that she caught young caterpillars and chewed them into balls which she put into the mouths of her young ones.

Since the larvae did almost nothing but eat, they grew rapidly. Soon they covered the doors of their cells with silk and turned into pupae. The pupae then became grown-up wasps that tore the silken doors open and crawled out of their cells.

The new wasps were workers which began to help their mother. Some cleaned out old cells, so eggs could be laid in them. Other workers chewed wood into paper and built rows of cells around the original nest. Workers also fed newly hatched larvae and stung a boy who poked the nest with a stick. All Pol had to do was get her own food and lay more eggs that hatched into still more workers.

When August came, Pol laid a few eggs that hatched into

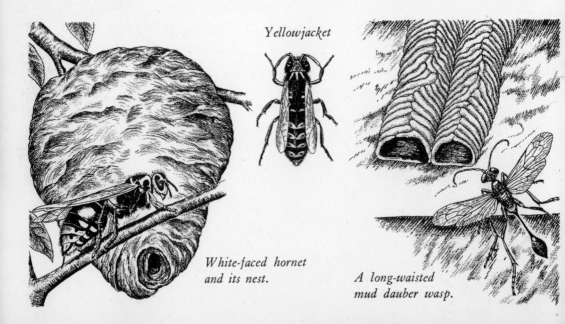

Yellowjacket

White-faced hornet and its nest.

A long-waisted mud dauber wasp.

special larvae. Some of them grew up to be male wasps, but others became queens like their mother. Instead of building cells or feeding larvae, these young queens and males mated with wasps from other nests.

By that time Pol was old and weak, and she died on the first frosty night of autumn. Then the workers and males began to die, too. At last only the young queens were left, and even they felt drowsy. Some of them hid in attics or in the garage, and one went to the hollow tree where Pol had stayed the year before. These young queens would sleep till spring sunshine would send them out to make nests of their own.

. . . . .

Wasps such as Pol are called Polistes (po liss' teez), for they have no everyday name. They are blackish, rust-colored, or black-and-yellow insects with waists that are neither long nor short. Their nests have just one layer of cells, with no covering around them.

Honey bees are divided into queens, males and workers. At the right is a honeycomb with ordinary cells and a special big one in which a queen is developing.

Worker   *Drone*   *Queen*

Yellowjackets are black-and-yellow wasps with short waists and powerful stings. Their nests contain several layers, or combs, and are covered with paper walls. Many of these nests hang in low trees or lie among weeds, but some kinds of yellowjackets build their nests in holes under ground.

White-faced hornets are big black-and-white wasps that nest in tall trees or on high buildings. Except for this, their nests resemble those of yellowjackets.

Bumblebees are another group of social insects that often build their nests underground. Their old queens, males, and workers also die in the fall. Only young queens live through the winter and start new colonies in the spring.

Honeybees live in hollow trees or in hives which people build for them. When winter comes, each queen sits in her hive and the workers gather around her in a ball. They also move to and fro and buzz their wings. This makes the insects so warm that they give off heat, just as you become hot when you run.

The bees' movements take a lot of energy, which is the power to do things. The workers get the energy they need by eating honey which is stored up during the summer. Men who keep bees always leave plenty of honey in the hives, so the insects can eat and keep warm during cold weather.

Queen honeybees that live in the North begin to lay eggs in March. Most of the eggs hatch and grow up into workers, but some become males and a few develop into queens. Queens and some males fly high into the air when they mate, but the males die soon afterward. Males that do not mate stay in the hives and are called drones. They are smaller than queens but larger than workers, and they cannot get their own pollen or nectar. Work-

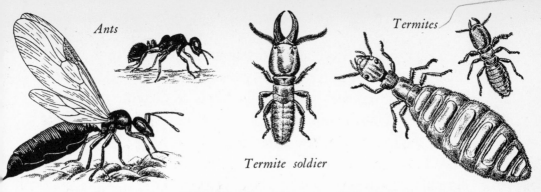

Ants

Termites

Termite soldier

Both ants and termites are social insects.

ers feed them when there is plenty of food, but when it is scarce the drones get nothing and sometimes starve.

Queen honeybees lay so many eggs that their hives become crowded. When that happens, the workers build some extra large cells that are irregular instead of six-sided. Larvae in these cells are fed a special kind of jelly that makes them grow up into queens. Just before the first new queen comes from her cell, the old one takes a lot of the workers and goes away to start another colony.

Ants are our commonest social insects, and they live almost everywhere. Some ants cut tunnels and rooms in tree stumps or in logs, but others dig homes in the ground. The insects pull out dirt with their jaws and take it to the surface. There they leave the dirt in cone-shaped piles. One common species makes piles twelve inches high and five or six feet wide.

Worker ants never develop wings, but queens and males have them. After a while these ants with wings fly about and mate. The males die, but the queens come down to the ground and lose their wings. After that, some queens lay eggs and take care of their first young ones, just as queen paper wasps do. Other queens join colonies of workers that are ready to take care of larvae. Several ant queens often live in a single nest.

Termites are important social insects, especially in tropical countries. We often call these creatures white ants, but their thick waists and soft bodies show that they are not ants.

Some termites feed on dead leaves, rotten wood, or tiny plants that live in the ground. Other kinds eat good, solid wood. When these wood-eaters get into buildings they eat through big timbers and boards, and even into furniture. The insects also eat books, since paper is made from wood.

Many termite colonies make their homes in the ground because the workers cannot live in dry air. Other colonies burrow into wood, and species that live in tropical countries build nests upon the ground or in trees. If the workers have to cross dry, open places, they build artificial tunnels by pasting grains of soil together. Air inside these tunnels is so moist that the termites live and work in comfort.

On damp, warm days in the spring or fall, thousands of termites come out of their nests and burrows. These insects are dark-colored, not white. The four wings with which they fly show that the termites are young males and queens.

These young insects fly about for a while—sometimes just a few minutes. Then they settle on the ground, where their wings break off. After that the males and females form pairs, and each pair digs a small room in the ground. There the queen lays a few small eggs that hatch into tiny nymphs, not larvae. When the nymphs grow up into workers, the new colony really begins.

Some Useful Insects

BOMBUS, a bumblebee worker, alighted upon a flower. It bent down under the weight of her big black and yellow body.

The flower was wide at its open end, but Bombus crawled far into it, where it became narrow. She had to do this to get to the place where she could suck sweet juice, or nectar. On the way she knocked off some yellow, powdery pollen. Some of it stuck to her fuzzy coat. After drinking all the nectar she could find, Bombus gathered still more pollen with her mouth and forelegs. Then she left the flower and buzzed away.

While Bombus was flying, she pushed the pollen back to her middle legs. Then she rubbed them together and put the pollen into two "baskets" on her hind legs. The "baskets" were made of long, curved hairs that grew around two smooth places. The hairs kept the pollen from falling off when Bombus crawled into another flower.

Some bumblebees make their homes in old mouse nests on the ground or in bushes, but many others use holes. Bombus's home was a hole that had once belonged to a chipmunk. When it went away, a bumblebee queen took the hole for her own.

When people move into an old, empty house, they always clean it. But the bumblebee queen did not bother to clean the chipmunk hole. Instead, she built a pot-shaped cell of wax and filled it with a mixture of nectar and pollen. Then she built a deeper cell, stored yellow pollen in it, and laid seven or eight eggs. Larvae that hatched from the eggs ate this pollen and honey which their mother brought them.

The larvae took about three weeks to grow, turn into pupae, and become worker bees. At first they were damp silver-gray creatures whose wings were too soft and weak for flying. The bees drank food from their mother's nectar pot, dried themselves, and became strong. After two or three days they were able to gather nectar and pollen and build new cells. Their mother still flew out of the nest now and then, but she did not work. All she had to do now was to lay more eggs that would hatch and grow up into still more bumblebees.

. . . .

Bombus was one of the first larvae that grew up to be workers. She built wax cells and fed her small, wriggly sisters. She was getting nectar and pollen for them when she crawled into flowers in the garden.

The worker bee got plenty of pollen—all her baskets would hold. But she did not get every grain, for some always fell on her coat. And some of those powdery grains were always brushed off when she crawled into another flower.

Though Bombus did not notice this, it was very, very important to the plants. For pollen is not just a yellow powder that is eaten by baby bees. Pollen "grains" are tiny bits of living material that make seeds develop. If Bombus and other insects did not carry pollen from flower to flower, many plants would never have seeds.

Pollen basket (empty)

Pollen basket (full)

This bumblebee is crawling into a flower to get nectar and pollen.

To make sure why pollen is so important, suppose we look at the parts of flowers and find out how they work. Most large blossoms have several outer parts that look like broad, bright-colored leaves. We think they are beautiful, but to insects they are signs that mean "Here is food!" Insects that see the bright-colored flowers go to them for pollen and nectar. Odors, which we often call perfumes, also are signals to insects. Many flowers that are small or even dull have odors that bring bees and other creatures to them.

At the center of each flower is a vase-shaped or bottle-shaped pistil, whose name is pronounced just as it is spelled. Around the pistil are stalked parts called stamens (stay' munz). Each pistil is a bit like a female insect, because it contains tiny eggs. The stamen, which produces pollen, takes the place of the male, or father. When pollen gets to the top of the pistil it grows down through the fleshy material of the plant until it reaches the eggs. There it makes them fertile, or able to grow. The eggs also become parts of seeds, which are covered with coats of various kinds, and even with thick, tasty fruits. When you eat a plum or an apple you are eating a fruit that has developed around one or several fertile eggs.

Seed-making in flowers would be easy if pollen from one blossom could fall upon its own pistil and fertilize its own eggs. But many seeds cannot start that way, and others will not be good if they do. The tiny eggs of most flowers must get pollen from other blossoms or even from other plants.

Pollen has two main ways of going from one plant to another. Many small flowers that have no nectar let their pollen float in the air. Breezes stir up millions of the tiny grains and often carry them for miles. Some of them fall on the ground and die, and others settle in swamps or lakes. But some are sure to drop on pistils and fertilize the eggs inside.

Pollen from sweet-smelling or bright-colored flowers travels in a different way. These blossoms contain sweet nectar, and their pollen also is good food. Insects come to suck nectar and to put pollen into their baskets. Of course, the insects also carry pollen

How a flower gets pollen, which makes seeds develop.

Pollen grows down
into a pistil until →
it fertilizes an egg.

Pollen

Pistil

Egg

A bumblebee carries
grains of pollen from
one flower to another.

from the stamens of one flower on their bodies, and brush it off onto the pistils of others. This begins the process of fertilization, which ends in the development of seeds.

. . . .

We have seen how Bombus, the bumblebee, takes pollen from one flower to another. Many kinds of flies, moths, butterflies, beetles, and even wasps also carry pollen from flower to flower. Most important of all are honeybees, which travel long distances to get pollen and nectar.

Of course, insects gather pollen and nectar for themselves and for their young ones, but in doing so they also help plants. Most of these plants are wild, but others grow in gardens and orchards. Many of our flowers come from seeds that were pollinated by insects. Apples, cherries, figs, and other fruits are insect-pollinated, and so are tomatoes, cucumbers, peas, beans, and pumpkins. Even chocolate "beans" develop after insects leave pollen on pistils.

We use fruits and vegetables that grow because insects carry pollen. We also use several insects, or things which they make. Bees, for example, make more honey than they and their larvae can eat. Human beings take the extra honey for food, and use wax which the bees build into cells. There is beeswax in candles, shaving cream, shoe polish, lipstick, floor wax, and many other everyday things.

Besides all this, farmers use bees to get bigger crops. Men who own orchards put beehives under the trees so the insects will carry pollen and make fruit develop. Farmers put beehives near fields of alfalfa so the plants will produce big crops of seed.

81

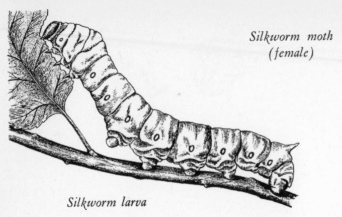
Silkworm larva

Silkworm moth
(female)

Cranberry growers also use bees to pollinate the flowers of their plants. One hive of bees on an acre will produce a fair crop, but three hives can produce a big one. If a cranberry grower has no bees of his own, he rents as many hives as he needs from a bee-keeper.

Lac insects are tiny creatures that live in southern Asia. They suck juice from trees and cover themselves with sticky, "gummy" material which soon becomes hard. When this material is cleaned and dissolved it becomes shellac. Shellac is used as a kind of varnish, as well as in linoleum, sealing wax, toothbrush handles, and so on.

Silkworms once lived wild in Asia, where they ate mulberry leaves and spun cocoons of grayish-white silk. They probably resembled cocoons spun by wild polyphemus caterpillars of North America.

About 4,500 years ago, someone in China discovered that silk from cocoons could be made into cloth. But wild cocoons were not always good, and it was hard to get enough of them. Silk "farmers" began to grow caterpillars in houses. As hundreds and thousands of years went by, the farmers raised cater-

Lac insects covered with hardened gum.

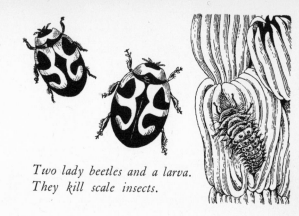

Two lady beetles and a larva. They kill scale insects.

Both lac insects and lady beetles are useful.

pillars that spun better and better cocoons. The moths' wings became smaller and smaller, too, till the males were hardly able to fly and the females could only flutter. While these changes were going on, the wild moths finally died out.

Silkworms were taken from China to Japan and to southern Europe. More and more caterpillars were raised, till in 1940 they produced 130 million pounds of silk. Then scientists learned how to make Nylon and other silky materials in factories. People liked these man-made substances, and began to use them instead of silk. Farmers still raise silkworms, but not nearly so many as were raised before Nylon became popular.

Perhaps the strangest way to use insects is to let them kill other insects. In California, for example, creatures called scale insects used to damage orange trees by sucking juice from their bark. Scientists found that a lady beetle from Australia ate the pests. When this lady beetle was brought to California it became so common and destroyed so many scale insects that the orange trees were saved.

Living in Winter

DANA, a monarch butterfly, sat on a small oak tree. When he spread his wings out in the sun, they were four inches wide.

Leaves of the oak tree were changing color, for autumn had begun. From a distance, Dana himself resembled an autumn leaf. The upper side of his wings was brownish orange, but the under side was lighter. The thick veins were black and so were the borders, with white and brownish spots. There were white spots on his thorax, too, but the rest of his body was black.

As Dana sat and sunned himself, he began to see other monarchs. At first they came in ones and twos, but then they arrived in dozens and hundreds. They flew over a hill and down to the grove where Dana was sunning himself. Soon they alighted around him and on nearby trees.

Dana had never seen so many monarchs, but he was not surprised. The time had come to migrate, or travel southward for the winter, and the butterflies were going in flocks. This special flock had been flying all day and was ready to stop for the night.

Dana slept with the other monarchs, and woke up when they did. Soon he began to fly with them, too. Up he went in curves and zigzags, until he was high above the trees. Then he turned and traveled southward with the other butterflies.

Dana was starting a long journey, but he did not have to hurry. He flapped his wings a few times and glided, over and over again. When he flapped his wings they pushed him forward. When he glided the air carried him along. Dana could fly this way all day long without becoming tired.

From time to time other butterflies joined the flock, till it seemed as if every monarch in the country had begun to migrate. They went on and on till late afternoon, but at last they stopped in another sunny place where they could rest on low trees. Monarch butterflies rested on those trees every year while they were traveling southward.

One morning, while the monarchs were flying, they found

The migrating monarch butterflies rested on oak trees.

themselves in trouble. A wind had come up from the west, and it blew harder and harder. Soon it began to push the butterflies eastward. Before noon, most of them had been forced away from the land and were flying above the ocean.

Dana had started out high up in the air, but he flew lower and lower. At last he was down close to the waves, where the wind did not blow too hard. There he was able to fly in zigzags that slowly took him back to the shore. When he got there, he found a clump of bushes and settled down to rest.

Other butterflies in the flock had as much trouble as Dana. Some were tossed to and fro until their wings were torn. A few were blown so far out to sea that they grew tired and fell into the water. The rest beat their wings up and down until they got back to the land. When they reached it, they hid from the wind and rested, just as Dana had done. There they stayed until the next morning, which was so sunny and calm that they could travel southward again.

Dana had joined the migrating monarchs near the coast of Massachusetts. Some of the other butterflies came from that state, too, but many had started out from Maine or from eastern Canada. The whole flock went southward along the Atlantic coast till it came to southern Florida. This meant that the butterflies from Canada traveled about 2,200 miles. Since Dana had started from Massachusetts, he flew only 1,600 miles.

While Dana was flying to Florida, flocks of monarchs also migrated across other parts of North America. Some came from farms and woods in the Middle West, or from western Canada. These butterflies went to low, warm places near the Gulf of Mexico. Other monarchs came from places near the Pacific coast

—some of them as far north as Alaska. Millions of these travelers went southward till they came to woods near the city of Monterey, California, and stopped to spend the winter there. Many butterflies from places not so far north went to Mexico.

Monarchs are the most famous of all butterfly migrants, but there are several others. Some red admirals fly to the South every fall, and so do some of their relatives which are known as painted ladies. Painted ladies live in both North America and Europe, and they sometimes migrate in huge flocks. The largest one ever

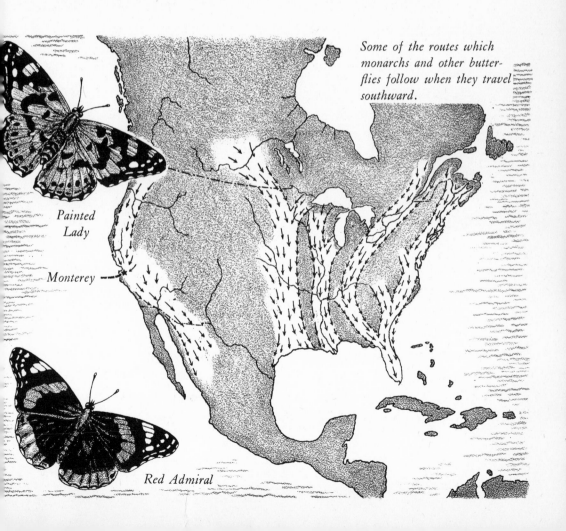

Some of the routes which monarchs and other butterflies follow when they travel southward.

Painted Lady

Monterey —

Red Admiral

This old monarch
flew northward in the spring.

Lady beetles
getting ready
to hibernate.

seen contained about three billion butterflies that went south-ward along the Pacific coast.

Birds that migrate southward in the autumn come back to their homes in the North next spring. Some monarchs also return to their northern homes. Most of these spring migrants are not young, handsome butterflies, as Dana was when he started for the South. They are old and tattered, instead, and they look as if they have traveled long distances. Still, we cannot be sure that they have come all the way from Florida or from the shores of the Gulf of Mexico.

Insects that live in the North and do not migrate spend the winter in various ways. Honeybees, as we know, stay in their hollow trees or hives and move to and fro to keep warm. But most bumblebees and wasps die in the fall. Only their queens go to sleep and so live until spring.

Winter sleep is called hibernation (hy ber nay' shun). Many beetles hibernate in burrows dug into the wood of trees, among dead leaves on the ground, or under bark and in other dark corners. Some beetles sleep alone, but others come together in swarms as soon as the weather turns cold. If you look in sunny

88

corners on autumn days, you may see hundreds of lady bugs that are getting ready to hibernate under rocks or in rotting logs. A scientist once found ten thousand lady bugs (which really are beetles) hibernating under a pile of dead leaves.

All mourning cloaks that live through the winter sleep in sheltered places. On warm days they often wake up and fly about or drink water that comes from melting snow. These butterflies have dark purplish-brown wings with blue spots and creamy borders.

Most moths and butterflies spend the winter as chrysalids or pupae. Butterflies generally fasten their chrysalids to plants, and moth pupae usually lie in cocoons that are spun on trees or weeds. But sphinx caterpillars wriggle into the ground before they turn into pupae. You can tell these pupae by the curved "handle," in which the tongue develops.

Woolly bears (page 94) are hairy black-and-brown caterpillars that grow up into tiger moths. When autumn comes,

Tent caterpillar eggs on a twig, a larva sleeping in a cornstalk, and a mourning cloak butterfly in a tree.

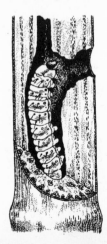

these caterpillars crawl about until they find hiding places under dead grass or leaves. There the caterpillars sleep until spring, when they spin cocoons and become pupae. Many other larvae hibernate, too. You may find them in cornstalks, in silken nests, or in shelters made of leaves. Dragonfly nymphs hide under plants and dead sticks in streams and ponds, and so do many water-dwelling larvae. Some of the nymphs stay awake all winter. They even catch food on warm days, but do not grow again until spring.

The best way of all to spend the winter is in the form of eggs. A mother insect can lay hundreds or even thousands of eggs, and can hide them easily. The eggs do not need food, and bad weather does not often kill them. When spring comes, the eggs hatch into nymphs or larvae that find plenty of food.

The tent caterpillar is a well-known insect that lives through the winter in eggs. Every summer, the mother moth lays 400 to 600 eggs in lumps, or clusters, around the twigs of trees. She covers each cluster with a brown crust that protects the eggs from freezing rain. When spring comes, the caterpillars hatch in time to eat the earliest, tenderest leaves. The caterpillars also spin tents of silk and rest in them at night or on stormy days.

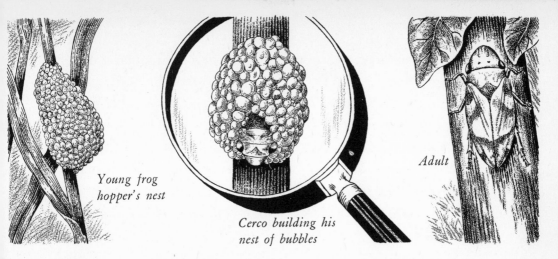

Young frog
hopper's nest

Cerco building his
nest of bubbles

Adult

Insects and the Weather

CERCO, the frog hopper, hatched one day in June. He came from an egg which his mother had laid in a stalk of grass.

Cerco was a tiny, yellowish creature with a broad, rounded head. His legs were short and thin, but he soon used them to crawl along the stem. After crawling a short distance, he stopped and sat with his tail up and his head downward. Soon he pushed his sharp beak into the stalk of grass and began to suck juice, or sap, from it.

Frog hoppers belong to the big group of insects that also includes aphids and cicadas. Leaf hoppers and tree hoppers belong to this group, too, and so do mealy bugs and scale insects like the one that is killed by lady beetles from Australia. All these creatures except the lady beetles feed by sucking sap from plants.

Soon after Cerco started to eat, bubbles began to form near his tail. They piled up higher and higher, until they made a bubbly nest that covered the baby frog hopper. The nest kept sunshine from harming his tiny, soft body. The bubbles also hid Cerco from other insects that would have liked to eat him.

Many people have wondered how frog hoppers get their bubbly nests. Some say they are made from spittle, and call the insects spittle bugs. Others think the nests are foam from the mouths of snakes or tree frogs, which explains the name frog hoppers. A few people have guessed that the nests "just happen" or ooze out of grass and weeds.

Anyone who watched Cerco closely could give the correct explanation. When Cerco drank sap, he mixed the liquid with chemicals produced in his body. These chemicals formed something like soap, which could be blown into bubbles.

At first the soapy liquid flowed from Cerco's abdomen. Then he began to raise and lower his tail. Raising it filled a pocket with air, but when the tail was lowered the air was pushed out, blowing a single bubble. Cerco pulled the bubbles forward along his back, until they covered him.

When we blow bubbles or make soapsuds, the bubbles soon disappear. But a frog hopper's soap is much tougher than ours, and its bubbles last very much longer. Cerco's first nest lasted four or five days. The next one he built remained moist and bubbly for one day more than a week.

Day and night Cerco sat in his nest, without trying to go outside. When he was hungry he sucked more sap, using it for food instead of blowing it into bubbles. But when he molted and grew larger, he left his old nest and made another one. He never tried to patch up an old nest and make it larger after it had become too small.

When Cerco molted for the last time, he became a full-grown insect with wings that were large enough to be used. He still sucked juice from plants, but instead of staying in a nest he flew from place to place. Between flights he rested on stems of grass or on weeds. There he always sat in the shade, where hungry birds could not find him.

. . . .

We human beings have red blood which also is very warm. It keeps us warm when the weather is chilly. Even in winter, when the weather is freezing, we do not become too cold.

Insects have thin, watery blood that generally is pale yellow or green. Insects' blood is not warm, and it cannot heat their bodies. An insect becomes very warm when the weather is hot and cools off when it becomes chilly. In the winter, insects that do not migrate or stay in the water become very, very cold. Only honeybees do not follow this rule, because they stay in their hives and "dance" to and fro to make heat.

Of course, an insect's body does not warm up as fast as the air around it, or cool off as quickly. This does not happen because the creature's coat takes up heat, or absorbs it, slowly. Then, after heat is absorbed, the coat keeps it from leaving the insect's body as soon as the air begins to grow cool. Insects also are so small that they can easily hide in shady spots when the sunshine becomes too hot, and they can snuggle down under warm stones as soon as evening comes.

Our fingers feel stiff when they are cold, and we cannot move them quickly. But most insects cannot move any part of their bodies quickly unless they are warm. A green darner dragonfly, for example, moves its wings 1,600 times per minute when it

93

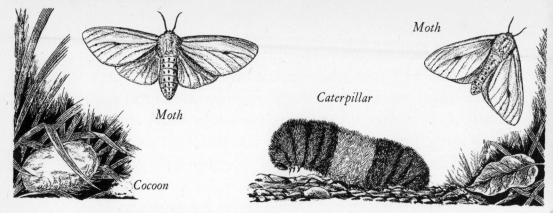

Woolly bear caterpillars apparently cannot predict mild or cold winters.

flies. A paper wasp beats its wings 6,000 times per minute, and a horse fly 20,000 times. But on a frosty morning not one of these creatures can move its wings fast enough to get into the air. At last the insects cannot even keep themselves alive. Both worker wasps and males die, though young queens hibernate. Most houseflies also die, but some sleep through the winter in attics, and begin to buzz about in the spring. Adult dragonflies die, of course. Their nymphs, which stay in the water, are almost too cold and dull to move.

Insects also are affected by light and by moisture in the air. Butterflies are active in sunshine, but most moths fly in the evening or at night. Some beetles will live only in dry places, but cockroaches stay where it is damp. When termites eat their way through dry wood, they always have tunnels that go into the ground. They let moisture from the ground go up to the places where the termites live.

Insects often feel changes in the weather before people notice them. Perhaps the insects do something different, too. When that happens, people use them as "signs" telling what the weather is going to be.

If you want to know how this can be done, suppose that you are a bee-keeper. One morning many of your bees do not leave their hives. Those that do fly away soon come back, and do not come out again. When you see this you tell your friends that it is going to rain. Probably it does rain, too.

Did the bees *know* it would rain? Of course not! Bees simply do not feel like flying about to get nectar in moist, cloudy weather. On this morning, many of the insects do not come out of their hives. Those that do come out go back when the air becomes more and more moist, or humid (hyu' mid). If you had noticed the weather, you could have said:

"It's cloudy this morning, and the air is becoming very moist. Rain often follows weather like this, so I think rain is coming." This prediction would be just as good as one that uses bees for "signs."

Many people think woolly bear caterpillars show what next winter's weather will be. These caterpillars, as we know, are black at both ends and reddish brown in the middle. If the brown band is very narrow, it is supposed to foretell a cold, snowy winter. If the band is very wide, the winter is supposed to be mild.

Scientists have begun to measure the brown color bands every fall and compare them with the next winter's weather. So far, there seems to be no real connection between the two. Color bands sometimes match the weather and sometimes do not. This means that the caterpillars really cannot tell what kind of winter is coming.

Other Books About Nature and Science

By CARROLL LANE FENTON

Life Long Ago: The Story of Fossils—The tale of "prehistoric" life from primitive sea plants to dinosaurs and Ice Age mammoths.
(*Children's Catalog.*)

Prehistoric World—Typical animals of the past 350 million years, how they looked, lived, and acted. (ALA *Booklist.*)

Earth's Adventures—The story of earth's long and adventurous past, and of the changes that are taking place upon it today. Illustrated by more than 130 drawings and photographs. (ALA *Booklist, Children's Catalog.*)

Weejack and His Neighbors—The stories of wild creatures that live on prairies of Canada and the United States. (ALA *Booklist.*)

Wild Folk at the Pond—Animal life in ponds and the small streams that flow into them. (ALA *Booklist, Children's Catalog.*)

Wild Folk in the Woods—"The kind of book...which the youngest child can listen to with profit and pleasure."
—*Charleston Evening Post.* (ALA *Booklist.*)

By CARROLL LANE FENTON *and* MILDRED ADAMS FENTON

Worlds in the Sky—"Scientific data, presented with graphic simplicity, highlight the pageantry of the sky."
—*Grade Teacher.* (ALA *Booklist, Children's Catalog.*)

Riches from the Earth—"An excellent book...about the rare and everyday riches that come from rocks in the earth." (*Children's Activities.*)

By CARROLL LANE FENTON *and* DOROTHY CONSTANCE PALLAS

Birds and Their World—"An introduction to many different birds and to the lives they lead...a fine book for elementary and junior high school."
—*Science Education* (ALA *Booklist, Children's Catalog.*)

By CARROLL LANE FENTON *and* HERMINIE B. KITCHEN

Plants That Feed Us—The story of grains and vegetables, from artichokes to zucchini, through almost 7000 years.